INTRODUCING COMPUTERS

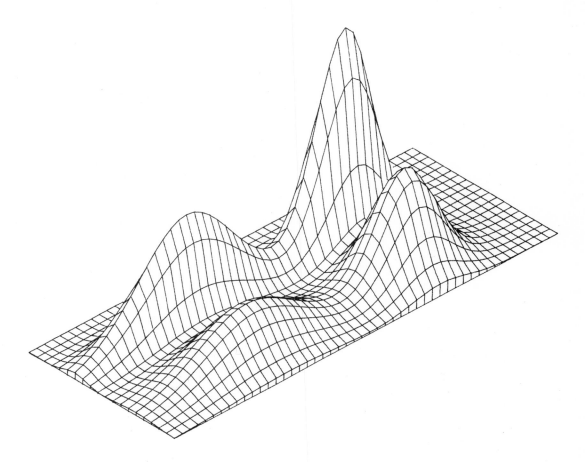

PETER BISHOP

NELSON

Thomas Nelson and Sons Ltd
Nelson House   Mayfield Road
Walton-on-Thames   Surrey KT12 5PL

P.O. Box 18123   Nairobi   Keyna

116-D JTC Factory Building
Lorong 3   Geylang Square   Singapore 1438

Thomas Nelson Australia Pty Ltd
19–39 Jeffcott Street   West Melbourne   Victoria 3003

Nelson Canada Ltd
1120 Birchmount Road Scarborough Ontario M1K 5G4

Thomas Nelson (Hong Kong) Ltd
Watson Estate   Block A   13 Floor
Watson Road   Causeway Bay   Hong Kong

Thomas Nelson (Nigeria) Ltd
8 Ilupeju Bypass   PMB 21303   Ikeja   Lagos

Phototypeset by Tradespools Limited, Frome, Somerset
Printed and bound in Hong Kong

The photograph on the cover, reproduced by kind permission of Dr
Jean Lorre and the Science Photo Library, shows a very modern
application of Computers. It is a picture of the spiral galaxy NGC
1097, enhanced by computer to reveal features not shown up by
normal telescopic methods. This technique is known as image
processing.

PREFACE

This book aims to provide a first introduction to computers. It is intended to be used by lower secondary school pupils, either as a preparation for an O-level or CSE course in Computer Studies, or as a complete course in its own right. It may also be used as a non-examination course for older pupils, and as a background reading for teachers, parents and any interested general readers.

The book assumes no previous knowledge of computers. The material is self-contained, but does link with other areas of knowledge at a very elementary level, such as electricity, binary numbers (no previous knowledge assumed), money (wages, accounts, gas bills etc.) and social and moral issues such as unemployment and peoples' rights to privacy.

The study of computers is a very broad subject, requiring a number of diverse skills. This book teaches the following skills:

● An appreciation of the nature, capabilities and limitations of computers.

● An appreciation of the role played by information in many contemporary activities, and the relationship between information and computers.

● An awareness, at an elementary level, of the structure of computers, and the way in which they work.

● An ability to write, run and correct simple programs on a computer, and to use programs already provided.

● An awareness of the jobs done by computers in industry, commerce, education and research, and the jobs done by people working with computers.

● An awareness of the way in which computers have developed.

● An appreciation of the effects that computers are having on society, both in Britain and elsewhere in the world.

Case studies are used quite frequently in the book, and these are of two types. Computer case studies outline some of the ways in which computers are used. 'People' case studies show some of the ways in which people work with computers, or can be affected by them. They are stories, written to be as realistic as possible, but they are not based on actual events. Any resemblance of the people described to actual people is entirely coincidental.

This book includes a number of 'package' programs. They are intended to be copied on to the school's computer, and then used by the pupils. The programs are written in a very simple subset of BASIC, and should work on the computers commonly available to schools. They have been tested on a Research Machines 380Z micro computer.

Cassette and disc versions of the packages are available for Research Machines 380Z and Commodore Pet microcomputers.

Acknowledgements

Aerofilms P. 137
Barclays Bank Limited P. 14 &113   Barnabys Picture Library P.1 (2 photos), P.3 (2 photos), P.6, P.11 (2 photos), P.13 (2 photos), P.22, P.24, P.31, P.32, P.43, P.91, P.108, P.111, P.120, P.126, P.133, P.137 (3 photos), P.138.   BBC Hulton Picture Library P.126, P.128, P.130, P.138 (2 photos).   Bell Fruit P.133   Benson Electronics P.23   Penni Bickle, V.R.U. P.13, P.56, P.109, P.110, P.125, P.140.   British Airways P.4, P.117   BBC Pictorial Publicity P.129   British Rail P.137
Dr Kenneth Brodlie, Leicester University, title page.
Colchester Lathe (Distributors) Limited P.2   John Collings and Partners P.14   Commodore Business Systems P.19
Dateline International P.123   Department of Transport P.119   Digital Equipment P.19, P.21, P.29, P.120
Mary Evans Picture Library P.127, P.128
Fiat Auto (UK) Limited P.118
Hoover Limited P.4
I.B.M. Limited P.1, P.6 (2 photos), P.14 (2 photos), P.15, P.19, P.21, P.22 (2 photos), P.23 (2 photos), P.24, P.105, P.106, P.108, P.147 (2 photos), P.151.   I.C.L. P.2, P.15 (2 photos), P.29, P.30, P.110.
Carolyn A Johns P.123
Michael Kaufmann, V.R.U. P.11, P.14, P.42, P.113, P.132 (2 photos)
Department for National Savings P.121, P.122   National Westminster Bank Limited P.113, P.133
Popperfoto P.130
Research Machines P.25   Chris Ridgers, V.R.U. P.3, P.18 (2 photos), P.91   Ann Ronan Picture Library P.125, P.128, P.130.
J. Sainsbury Limited P.22   Science Museum P.126, P.130 (2 photos), P.131, P.135 (2 photos), P.132   J.J. Silber Limited P.133   Space Frontiers P.27
Tilbury Sandford Brysson Limited P.2   Time and People Limited P.113   Times Newspapers Limited P.76
University Computing Centre, Dundee P.4

CONTENTS

CHAPTER I

INTRODUCTION: A FIRST LOOK AT COMPUTERS

Computers are everywhere. You can find them in offices, factories, shops, hospitals, schools, ships, satellites and even in some people's homes. Their numbers are increasing all the time. Some people like computers, other people hate computers. Unfortunately, many people do not know much about them.

This book gives you a first look at computers. It tells you a little about how they work, how they are used and how they have developed. It teaches you how to use a computer yourself. It also tells you about some of the effects, both good and bad, that computers are having on society.

This chapter, the introduction, concerns two very important questions:

- What is a computer?
- What can and can't a computer do?

In the process of answering these questions, computers are compared with a number of everyday objects, with which you are probably quite familiar. Computers are similar in several ways to washing machines, lathes, traffic lights and pocket calculators. This should start to remove some of the mystery which surrounds computers.

WHAT IS A COMPUTER? There is quite a lot to this question. In this chapter, it is answered in three stages. At the end of the book, there is another look at the question.

FIRST ANSWER: A COMPUTER IS A MACHINE The sewing machine, lathe and computer are all devices which do things. Like a sewing machine and a lathe, a **computer is a machine**.

However, there are some important differences. A lathe cuts and shapes metal, and a sewing machine stitches cloth. On the other hand, a computer can do more than one type of work. A computer is much more versatile than a lathe or a sewing machine.

The machines shown in the photographs below use electricity. But there is an important difference between the computer circuits and the hairdryer. The hair dryer has moving parts inside it. On the other hand, a computer has no moving parts inside it. It works entirely by the behaviour of the electrons, which make up electricity, as they travel through its circuits. For this reason, **a computer is an electronic machine**.

SECOND ANSWER: A COMPUTER IS AN ELECTRONIC MACHINE

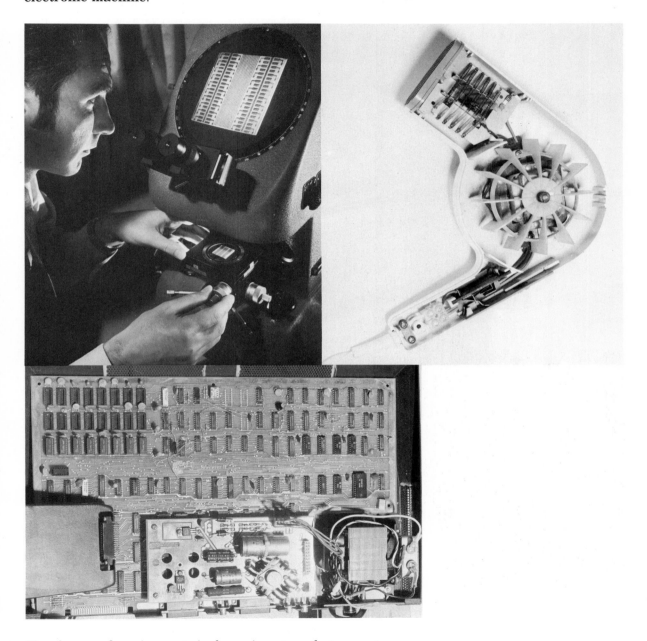

The absence of moving parts is the main reason that computers can work so quickly.

THIRD ANSWER: A COMPUTER IS AN AUTOMATIC MACHINE

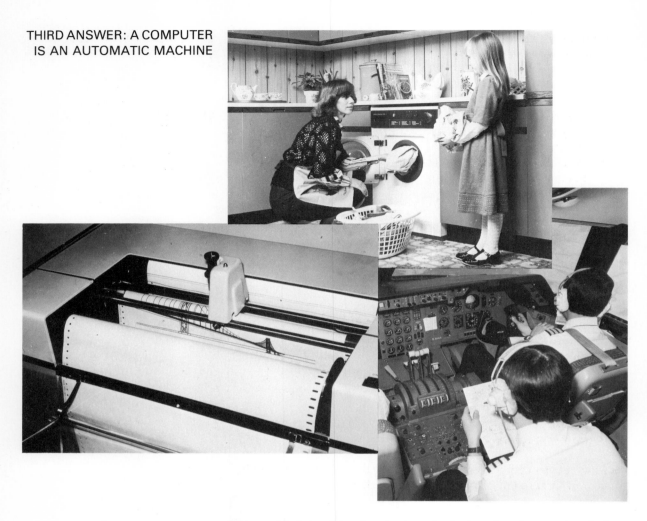

The washing machine has just washed, rinsed and spun the clothes automatically. The automatic pilot is keeping the aeroplane on course without the pilot having to do anything. The computer has just finished drawing a plan of a suspension bridge all by itself. Like an automatic washing machine and an aeroplane automatic pilot, **a computer is an automatic machine**.

But how do these automatic machines know what to do? The answer is that they are instructed. An automatic washing machine is told how many times to wash, rinse and spin the clothes, and how long to take. An automatic pilot is set to keep a certain course. Before a computer can start doing a piece of work, all the instructions which tell it what to do are stored inside it. These instructions are called a **program**.

It is important to remember that a computer can do a much wider range of work than either an automatic washing machine, or an automatic pilot. In other words, a computer can run a very wide variety of programs.

A computer is an automatic, electronic machine. A computer can perform a wide variety of tasks. Each task follows a set of instructions called a program.

1 Answer these questions from the text you have just read:
   a Why is a computer called an electronic machine?
   b What is a program?
   c What is the main difference between a computer and an automatic pilot?
   d Do computers contain moving parts?
   e Are computers very scarce?

2 Look at this list of machines and devices:

traffic lights   digital watch
photograph booth   typewriter
television set   film projector
pocket calculator   guitar amplifier

Write down the ones which are:
a automatic
b electronic

It is hard to decide about one or two of them. Discuss these.

3 A computer needs a program to tell it what to do. So does an automatic washing machine. Write down a list of some other machines or devices which can be programmed.

4 Find out where the nearest computer to your school is. What kind of work does it do? Try to arrange to visit it.

You hear all sorts of stories about what computers can do, or have done. Unfortunately, not many of them are true. This section is about the capabilities and limitations of computers – what can and can't a computer do?

WHAT CAN AND CAN'T A COMPUTER DO?

Computers can do a wide variety of tasks. Just a few of them are shown in the photographs on the next page. In fact, many of these tasks could be carried out by the same computer. What do these tasks have in common?

Some of the tasks shown in the photographs on page 6 involve calculations. As most people realise, computers can calculate. These calculations can be extremely complicated. On the other hand, many computers spend much of their time doing very easy calculations over and over again. It is the very high speed and extreme accuracy of computers that makes them suited to calculations of all types.

CALCULATIONS

INFORMATION PROCESSING

Computers can do much more than calculate. For example, calculating wages involves knowing such information as hours worked, pay rate and income tax code. Computers can look up this information. Making airline seat reservations requires several items of information: details of the flight, whether there are any seats available, etc. In fact, all the tasks shown in the photographs are concerned with information.

Information is the key to the question: '**What can computers do?**' A brief answer to this question is:
Computers process information

Calculating is only one type of information processing. Other types are storing, sorting and locating information, and bringing information up to date. Some of these processes involve making simple decisions like 'which of two numbers is larger?' Computers can make decisions of this sort, but **computers cannot think for themselves**.

Remember that everything a computer does is in response to instructions in a program.

What kind of information can a computer process?
Computers can do a wide variety of tasks. This means that they must process many kinds of information. Information which computers can process includes numbers, names, addresses, codes and passages of writing. The information is always made up of figures, letters or punctuation marks. This is why computers are sometimes called **digital computers**. Digital computers cannot process sounds or pictures directly.

A computer is an information processing machine. Information processing includes storing, locating, and sorting information, doing calculations, and making simple decisions. The information which computers process is made up of figures, letters and punctuation marks.

Computers cannot think for themselves. They can only follow program instructions.

ONCE AGAIN: WHAT CAN AND CAN'T A COMPUTER DO?

EXERCISE

1 Answer these questions from the text you have just read:
  a Can a computer process sounds directly?
  b Why are computers suited to doing repetitive calculations?
  c Can the same computer do more than one kind of information processing task?
  d Could a computer decide whether murderers should be hanged?
  e Do all computers spend most of their time doing complicated calculations?

2 Decide which of these tasks you think a computer could be programmed to do:
  predict the winner of this season's F.A. Cup
  calculate a person's income tax
  forecast tomorrow's weather
  control a rocket
  decide who will win if there is a Third World War
  translate a book from one language to another
  decide whether war is a bad thing

  Some of these are quite difficult to decide. Discuss them.

3 Write a list of tasks which you think a computer cannot be programmed to do.

4 Find out from other people, who are not studying computers, what they think computers can and cannot do. Discuss your findings.

INFORMATION IN AND OUT

You have already learned that a computer is an automatic, electronic machine which processes information. In order to process information, a computer must be supplied with the information in the first place. Large quantities of information are often involved. In a similar way, when a computer has finished processing, it must supply the results of the processing. Many computer applications require a flow of information to and from the computer while processing is taking place.

To get information in and out of a computer, there are operations called **input** and **output**. Input is the operation of supplying information to a computer. Output is the operation of printing or displaying information that has been processed by a computer. As you will see later in the book, computers include devices to carry out the operations of input and output.

Most computer programs include instructions for all three types of operation: input, processing and output. Before a computer can run a program, the program itself must be input into the computer.

The ideas of input and output raise the point that a computer cannot work completely on its own. **People** are required to collect and prepare information to be input. Computer output is designed to be used by people. Also, people write the programs which tell a computer what to do.

SOME EXAMPLES OF INPUT, PROCESSING AND OUTPUT

If you think about it, you will realise that many everyday tasks have input, processing and output stages. A few examples of these tasks are given here. Thinking about a task in terms of input, processing and output often makes the task easier to understand. It also helps when writing a program to carry out a task, as you will see in a later chapter.

Example 1 – Making milkshake
A recipe for vanilla milkshake is:

Ingredients:
    1 cup chilled fresh milk
    ¼ cup powdered milk
    ½ cup vanilla ice cream
    2 teaspoons sugar
    ⅛ teaspoon vanilla flavouring

Instructions:

Place all the ingredients in a bowl.	**(Input)**
Beat with an egg beater until smooth.	**(Processing)**
Pour into a large glass and serve.	**(Output)**

The input, processing and output steps are fairly obvious.

Example 2 – A bus conductor

The job of a bus conductor is to:

Ask each passenger where he or she is going.	**(Input)**
Look up the fare if necessary.	**(Processing)**
Tell the passenger the fare.	**(Output)**
Collect the money.	**(Input)**
Work out the change.	**(Processing)**
Issue the tickets and the change.	**(Output)**

In this example, each step occurs twice.

These examples show that it is not only computers which have input, processing and output stages to their work.

A WORD OF CAUTION: GARBAGE IN, GARBAGE OUT

Stories of computers producing million pound gas bills are quite common, and sometimes true. But it is also true that computers hardly ever make mistakes. How is it, then, that computers sometimes output wrong information?

In most cases the problem is with the input information. If input information is wrong, the output it produces will also be wrong. There is a saying for this in the computer world: **Garbage In, Garbage Out**. It is sometimes shortened to **GIGO**.

Most computer programs test all input information, and reject any which is obviously wrong. But it is impossible to detect every item of wrong information.

END-OF-CHAPTER SUMMARY

This chapter has introduced a number of very important ideas:

- A computer is an automatic, electronic information processing machine.

- A program is a set of instructions to a computer. Everything a computer does is in response to program instructions.

- Information processing includes storing, locating and sorting information, doing calculations and making simple decisions.

- Getting information in and out of a computer requires input and output operations respectively.

- Many tasks, not only ones done by computers, can be described in terms of input, processing and output steps.

- Garbage In, Garbage Out.

The rest of the book develops these ideas. You will learn more about how computers work, how they are used, how to program a computer yourself, and how computers are affecting society.

1 Answer these questions from the text you have just read:

   a Can a computer work completely on its own?

   b What is input?

   c Is the output from a computer always correct?

   d What is the most common reason for wrong output?

  ·e How often do computers make mistakes?

2 Identify the input, processing and output stages of these tasks:

   a Working at a till at a supermarket:

     Enter the price of each item.

     Ring up the total.

     Tell the customer the amount.

     Collect the money.

     Work out the change.

     Give the change and the receipt.

   b Developing a film:

     1 Place the film in its holder, and both in the developing tank.

     2 Add the developing fluid.

     3 Leave until the correct time has elapsed, agitating the film at regular intervals.

     4 Pour off the developing fluid.

     5 Repeat steps 2, 3 and 4 using the stop bath, then the fixing fluid.

     6 Rinse the film for at least 30 minutes in running water.

     7 Carefully remove the holder from the tank, and the film from the holder, and hang the film up to dry.

3 Investigate other tasks which you think involve input, processing and output stages. Write down the steps of each task, and identify the input, process and output steps.

4 Discuss how your ideas about what a computer is, and what a computer can and cannot do, have changed while you have worked through this chapter.

CHAPTER 2

INFORMATION AND COMPUTERS

In the previous chapter you learned that a computer is an information processing machine. This chapter takes a closer look at information. You will learn (if you have not noticed already) how much information there is all around us. Your attention is drawn to some of the problems of keeping large quantities of information. Finally you will be introduced to some of the ways in which information is stored on computers.

Information stored on paper takes up a lot of room

THE WORLD OF INFORMATION

Everything we see, hear, feel, smell and taste is information. Most of the time we are receiving far more information than we can cope with. We can only remember a tiny amount of all the information which reaches us.

Some of this information is natural, like the colour of the sky. But these days more and more information is man-made. Modern society depends on vast quantities of information. It has been said that man the hunter has evolved into man the information gatherer.

The photographs at the beginning of the chapter show a few examples of large quantities of information. Many activities depend on such large quantities of information. For example, telephones would not be much use without telephone directories. Banks depend on records of money put in and taken out by their customers. Builders rely on architect's plans when constructing buildings. There are many more examples.

Storing information has its problems. The information must be accurate and up-to-date. Items of information must be easy to find. For these reasons, large stores of information are always kept in some sort of order. For example, telephone directories are kept in alphabetical order, or it would be impossible to find someone's number. Banks keep their accounts in order of account numbers.

Other problems arise when the information is kept about people. These problems are discussed in Chapter 12.

EXERCISE

1   Answer these questions from the text you have just read:
    a   Does modern society depend on information?
    b   List some sources of information mentioned in the text.
    c   When large quantities of information are stored, does the order of storage matter? Why?
    d   Name one source of information which is kept in alphabetical order.

2   In what order do you think each of the following collections of information are kept?
    Words in a dictionary
    Bank accounts
    Lists of flights from an airport
    Recipes in a cookery book
    Parts lists at a factory
    Cards in a library catalogue

3   State what information you think is needed when:
    Someone needs a blood transfusion.
    An aeroplane approaches an airport to land.
    You try to find a radio station on your radio.
    A cheque is cashed.
    You choose a new pair of curtains for a room.
    You walk across a street.

4   Find out as many activities as you can which need large amounts
    of information.

5   How many items of information can you see in this photograph?

INFORMATION AND DATA

We now turn our attention to information and computers. Can
computers process any type of information? Most certainly not. The
photographs above show the sort of information which can be
processed by computers, and the sort which cannot.

Computers can only work with information which is represented in
certain ways, usually as numbers or letters. Sometimes the
information is in a code. In many cases information must be specially
prepared before it can be processed by a computer. Information which
computers use is called **data**. The work of a computer is often
described as **data processing**.

Vague information cannot easily be made into data. For example, if you ask someone 'How tall are you?' and the person replies 'Quite tall.', this is too vague to be put onto a computer.

DATA STORAGE

There are special ways of storing data:

- ready for input into a computer.
- inside a computer.

Some of these ways are now discussed.

Data ready for input into a computer

The photograph on the left shows a tag which many shops attach to their goods. When an item is sold, its tag is removed, and sent to the shop's computer. The tag contains data about the item, such as its price, size and colour. The data is coded by means of the holes in the tag. An input device can read this data into the computer.

Other methods of storing input data include punched cards, paper tape, bar codes, magnetic ink characters, and printed characters which can be read directly. The photographs below show data stored in these ways.

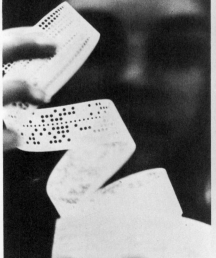

Above   *Kimball tag*
Right   *Magnetic ink characters on a cheque*
Bottom left   *Paper tape*
Centre   *Bar code on a soft drink*
Bottom right   *Punched cards*

Cheque No.	Branch No.	Account No.

⑅039806 ⑅20⑅9993⑆ 10324965⑅

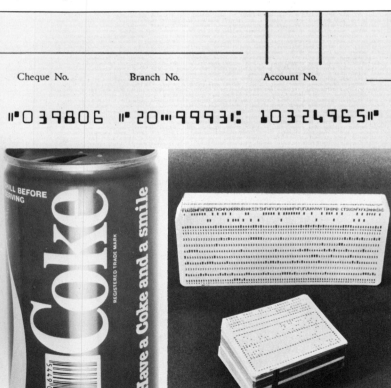

14

Data stored inside a computer

After data has been input into a computer, it is again stored. There are several methods of storage, including magnetic tapes, magnetic discs and the memory of the computer. The photographs below show these methods of storing data.

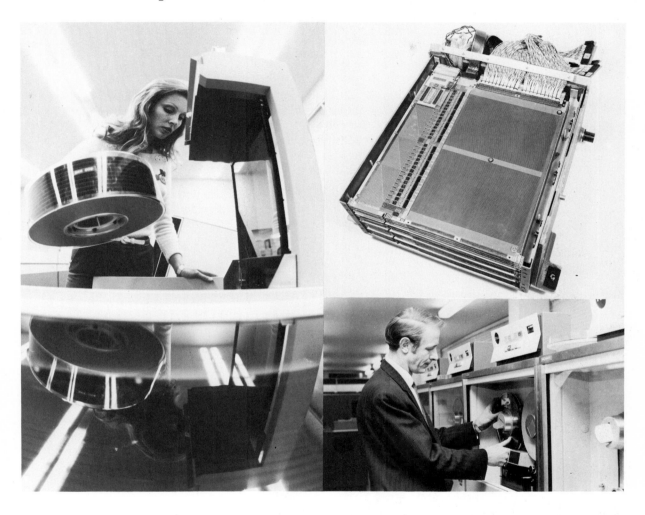

All data stored inside a computer is in code. Different codes are often used in different parts of the computer, but all these codes have one thing in common. They use the digits 0 and 1 only. This is because 0 and 1 are the easiest digits to store and process in computers. The digits 0 and 1 are called **bits**.

But why is it easiest to have only 0 and 1? Well, computers, like lights, work by electricity. A light can be switched on or off. Similarly, a circuit in a computer can be switched on or off, to store a 1 or a 0. The magnetic tapes and magnetic discs used by computers have many small spots. These spots can be magnetised in one direction or another. In this way, each spot can store a 0 or a 1.

Left   *Magnetic disc pack*
Top right   *Memory circuits*
Bottom right   *Magnetic tape drive*

BINARY NUMBERS   How can we represent numbers, letters and other characters using only 0 and 1? With numbers the answer is quite easy – use **binary numbers**.

Ordinary numbers are written as units, tens, hundreds, etc. Binary numbers are written as units, twos, fours, eights, etc. For example:

ordinary (decimal) number: 13 = 1 ten and 3 units
binary number: 1101 = 1 eight, 1 four, no twos
                                      and 1 unit
                                  = 13 (decimal)

Here are the first ten binary numbers:

decimal	binary
1	1
2	10
3	11
4	100
5	101
6	110
7	111
8	1000
9	1001
10	1010

So it is (almost) true to say that numbers inside a computer are coded in binary. (Not quite true, though, because negative numbers and very large numbers need special treatment.) In all cases, however, only the digits 0 and 1 are used.

What about letters and characters? They are also stored as combinations of 0's and 1's. Occasionally the codes for letters and numbers get mixed up, as inside a computer they are very similar.

Storage capacities
Some of the storage methods mentioned in this chapter can store very large quantities of information. For example:

- One punched card can store 80 characters.

- One inch of paper tape stores 10 characters.

- One reel of magnetic tape stores up to 50 million characters.

- One pack of magnetic discs stores up to 300 million characters.

Here are the main points introduced in this chapter:

- We live in a world which depends on large quantities of information.

- To be of any use, information must be stored in some order.

- Information which can be used by computers is called data.

- Data can be stored in several ways both outside and inside computers.

- All data stored in computers is in codes. These codes use the digits 0 and 1 only.

- Binary numbers are numbers which use the digits 0 and 1 only.

1   Answer these questions from the text you have just read:

   a   What is data?
   b   Can computers store all kinds of information?
   c   Name one kind of information which cannot be stored by a computer.
   d   Name some ways of storing data ready for input into a computer.
   e   Name some ways of storing data inside a computer.
   f   Which digits represent all data stored in a computer? Why is this?
   g   Are all numbers inside a computer stored in binary?

2   Here is a piece of paper tape storing the word COMPUTER:

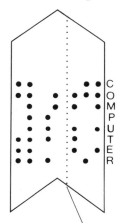 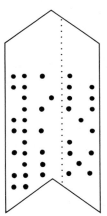

These small holes guide the tape.
They are not part of the code.

a   What word is punched on the other piece of tape? (You will have to guess one letter.)
b   Draw a piece of tape containing the word TRUMPET.

3 Have you noticed any shops which use Kimball tags? Make a list of these shops.

4 Write down the binary numbers from 11 to 20.

5 One way of storing numbers on a computer is to code each decimal digit separately in binary. For example:

```
3        6        7
|        |        |
0011    0110    0111
```

   a Code the decimal numbers 513 and 999 in this way.
   b What decimal number is coded as 0100 0010 1000?
   c What is one disadvantage of coding numbers in binary?

6 Sam the spy has a secret method for passing information to his partner (who is also his milkman). Sam puts his empty milk bottles in a box. His box can contain up to three bottles. His code depends on the number of bottles he puts out, and their positions in the box. Here are two examples:

Beware, you are being followed   *Nothing to report*

   a Sketch all the other combinations of bottles Sam can put out. Provide a suitable message for each combination.
   b Can you think of another (shorter) way of representing the same code?
   c How can the milkman reply to Sam's messages?

7 Make up a secret code of your own.

CHAPTER 3
THE PARTS OF A COMPUTER

At this stage, you have learned a number of things about computers. Here are the most important facts again:

- Computers can store and process large quantities of information, more properly called **data**.

- Working with data requires three operations: These are **input**, **processing** and **output**.

- Computers work automatically: They are told what to do by sets of instructions called programs.

This chapter introduces the parts of a computer which do these tasks. As you can see from the photographs, computers vary considerably in size. Small computers, sometimes called **microcomputers**, have most of their parts in a single box, or **unit**. Large computers are made up of a number of separate units.

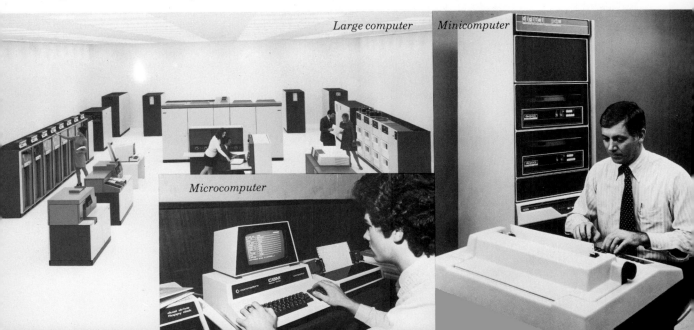

Large computer   *Minicomputer*

Microcomputer

OVERALL STRUCTURE OF A COMPUTER

Whether they are separate units, or all in one unit, all computers contain the parts shown in the diagram below:

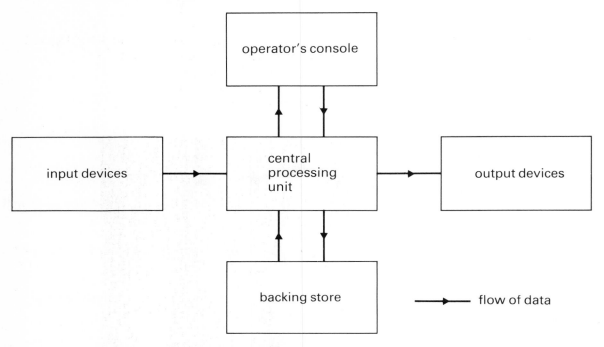

Block structure of a computer

From the diagram you can see that a computer consists of a number of devices. These devices work together to input, process and output information.

This leads to the important idea of a **system**. A system is a collection of parts working together. People can be parts of a system. Because they consist of a number of devices working together, computers are sometimes called systems.

The components which make up a computer are called **hardware**. Hardware includes the electronic circuits, wires, switches, magnets and other devices found in a computer.

EXERCISE

1 Answer these questions from the text you have just read:
   a What is a unit?
   b What is a system?
   c Do all computers contain a number of units?
   d Why is a computer sometimes called a system?
   e What is hardware?

2 Some examples of systems are: a motor car, a rugby team, a city. Write down some more examples.

Each of the parts of a computer shown in the diagram on page 20 is now described in a little more detail.

The CPU is where processing of information takes place. It consists entirely of electronic components called **chips**, and has no moving parts. Some computers have their complete CPU in one chip. These chips are called **microprocessors**.

A CPU consists of three parts, as shown in the diagram below.

THE CENTRAL PROCESSING UNIT, OR CPU

control unit
arithmetic and logic unit
memory

The parts of a central processing unit

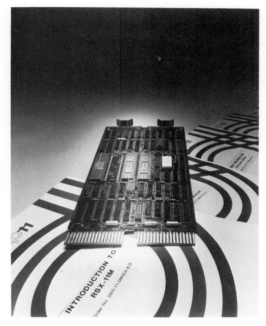

Part of the CPU of a microprocessor

The **memory**, or **main store** holds the programs and the data which a computer is using at the time. In older computers, the memory consisted of small metal rings, called **ferrite cores**. These can be magnetised in one direction or another to store a 0 or a 1.

In modern computers, the memory is made of electronic components like the rest of the CPU.

The memory of a computer consists of a number of **cells**. Each cell contains one item of data, or one program instruction. The contents of any memory cell can be examined, or replaced, at any time.

An old-fashioned computer memory made of ferrite cores

The **arithmetic and logic unit**, or **ALU**, is where calculations are done, decisions are made and other data processing operations are carried out.

The **control unit** controls the order in which program instructions are carried out. It is also responsible for the timing of all the operations done in the CPU.

INPUT DEVICES

Ways of storing input data were mentioned in the previous chapter. Input devices read data or programs and feed them into a computer.

There are many different kinds of input devices. These include punched card readers, paper tape readers, bar code readers, magnetic ink character readers and special devices to read Kimball tags. Most computers have several input devices.

Left   *Bar code reader in a supermarket*
Centre   *Paper tape reader*
Right   *Punched card reader*

A type of input method which is being developed at the moment is **voice recognition**. It may soon be possible to speak instructions or data to a computer.

Having read the input data, input devices send the data, now coded as 0's and 1's, to the CPU of the computer.

Right   *Dr Fred Jelinek and Dr Alan Cole, two of the pioneers of computer voice recognition, experimenting with their equipment.*

Output devices print or display information which has been processed by a computer. The commonest output device is a **line printer**. A line printer can print data very quickly – one line at a time, in fact. Other output devices include visual display units, graph plotters and graphics display units. Graphical output is one of the fastest growing areas of computing.

Special cameras can be used to produce **computer output on microfilm (COM)**. A number of pages of output are reduced in size onto a single piece of film. A special microfilm reader is used to read the data. Computer output on microfilm saves large quantities of paper.

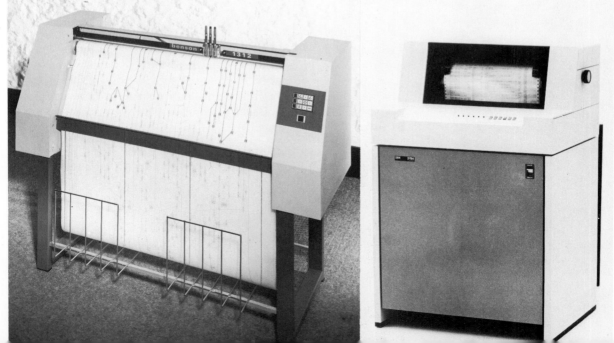

Top left   *Graphics display unit*
Bottom left   *Graph plotter*
Bottom right   *Line printer*

Top   *Magnetic tape units*
Bottom *Magnetic disc drives*

The main store inside the CPU of a computer is usually too small to contain all the programs and data the computer might want to use. Extra space for programs and data is provided by **backing store**. The commonest backing store units are **magnetic tape units** and **magnetic disc drives**. Backing store can hold very large amounts of data.

One often hears of **data banks**, which are large amounts of information that can be accessed by computers. Data banks are kept on the backing store of computers.

OPERATOR'S CONSOLE

The operator's console is often attached to the CPU of a computer. It enables the computer to be started and stopped, programs to be loaded and run, and messages to be sent to the person operating the computer.

Speeds of data storage devices

The devices which make up computers work at very different speeds. Here are some typical examples:

Card reader	**inputs** 400 cards per minute which is 500 characters per second
Line printer	**outputs** 400 lines per minute which is 800 characters per second
Magnetic tape drive	**reads or writes** 50 000 characters per second
Magnetic disc drive	**reads or writes** 500 000 characters per second
CPU	**processes** 1 000 000 instructions per second.

Remember that these figures are only approximate, and are improving all the time.

These differences in speed cause considerable problems. Ways of overcoming these problems are discussed in Chapter 6.

PUTTING THE UNITS TOGETHER

In medium and large sized computers, each unit is separate. The units are connected by a number of wires which run under the floor of the computer room. The computer can be expanded by adding new units, or modified by replacing units. Some very large computers have more than one CPU.

The smallest computers, called **microcomputers**, have a processing unit, attached to a keyboard and a visual display screen. How do these units do all the tasks mentioned earlier? The keyboard is the input device, and the operator's console. The screen shows input and output. The processing unit contains a microprocessor. If there is any backing store, it is a cassette tape recorder or floppy disc drive connected to the processing unit.

Microcomputer

The cost of computers

One of the main reasons for the popularity of computers is their cost. Computers are cheap, and are getting cheaper all the time. This is especially important because just about everything else is getting more and more expensive.

Here are some costs for five similar medium sized computers, bought between 1962 and 1979.

Year	Cost	Cost at 1962 prices
1962	£172 000	£172 000
1966	£128 000	£112 000
1969	£ 95 000	£ 73 000
1973	£ 91 000	£ 53 000
1979	£ 69 000	£ 17 000

The middle column shows what the computers cost at the time when they were bought. The last column shows what the costs would have been if there had been no inflation since 1962. (Figures from Computer Weekly, 15th December 1979)

EXERCISE

1 Answer these questions from the text you have just read.
   a Where in a computer does processing take place?
   b What is a microprocessor?
   c What is a microcomputer?
   d What are the parts of a CPU?
   e State whether each of the following devices are input, processing, backing store or output devices:
      memory, punched card reader, magnetic disc drive, ALU.
   f How are data banks stored?

2 Use the speeds of the devices mentioned in the text to do these calculations, concerning a set of data containing 1 million characters.
   a How long will it take to read the data from punched cards?
   b How long will it take to store the data on magnetic tape?
   c How long will it take to store the data on a magnetic disc?

3 Identify the units in the computers shown in the photographs at the beginning of this chapter. Find some other photographs of computers from newspapers or magazines, and identify the units.

4 Using the cost figures mentioned in the text, draw a graph of the costs of the computers at the different times. Extend your graph to predict the cost of a similar computer in 1983 and 1987.

CHAPTER 4
COMPUTERS AND COMMUNICATIONS

Computers are concerned with processing information. Communications networks, like telephones, radio and television, are concerned with sending information from one place to another. Computers can very often provide the right information for a particular purpose, but at the wrong place. Combining computers with communication systems provide the right information, at the right place, at the right time. One of the biggest steps forward in the development of computers has been their combination with telephone, radio and television networks.

This chapter introduces some of the ways in which computers can be combined with communication systems. Mention is made of the hardware used, and of ways in which long-distance computing is applied.

Communications Satellite

TERMINALS A device which provides a direct link with a computer is called a **terminal**. A terminal can be right next to the computer with which it connects, or it can be miles away. Long distance links between terminals and computers are provided by telephone lines, radio links or communications satellites. This enables the computer to be thousands of miles from the terminal.

Terminals can be used for input and output of data. The block diagram below shows how they relate to the other parts of a computer.

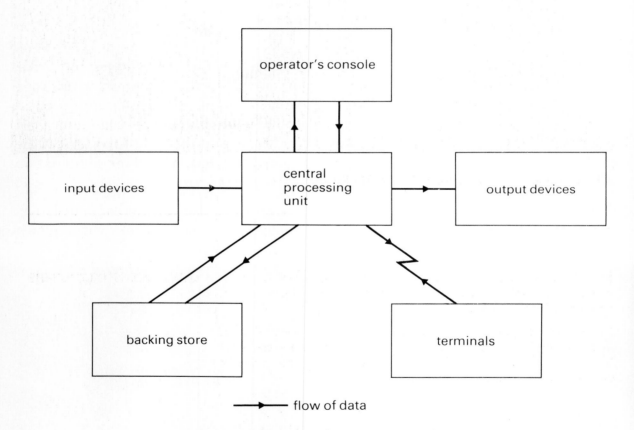

Block diagram of a computer with terminals

The commonest types of terminals are **teletypes** and **visual display units**, or **VDU's**. Both have keyboards like typewriters. In a teletype, the input and output data is printed on paper. In a VDU, the data is displayed on a screen, rather like a television screen.

Many computer installations have replaced their card readers and paper tape readers with terminals. These terminals are only used for input of data. This method of data input is called **direct data entry**.

28

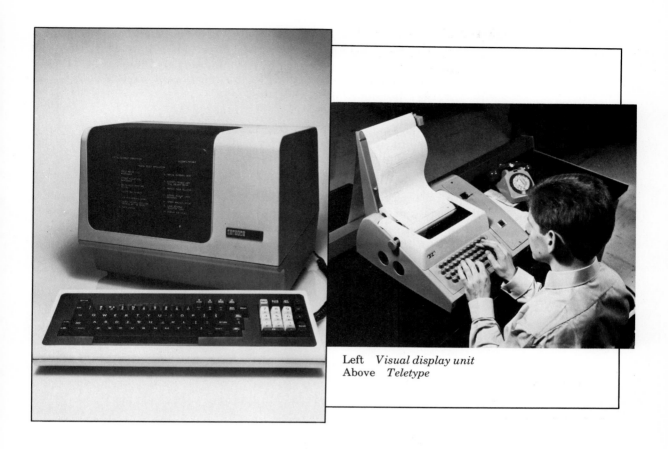

Left   *Visual display unit*
Above   *Teletype*

In addition to linking terminals to computers, communications systems can link computers to other computers. In this way, networks of computers are formed.

Networks of computers have several advantages. All the work to be done is shared amongst the computers. This prevents one computer from being overloaded while others stand idle. If one computer breaks down, then its work is transferred to another.

NETWORKS OF COMPUTERS

Speeds of terminals
Speed of input from a terminal: up to 10 characters per second (as fast as a person can type).

Speed of data along a telephone line: between 30 and 100 characters per second on an ordinary line, much higher on a special line.

Speed of output at a terminal: between 30 and 100 characters per second.

APPLICATIONS

Computers with terminals have a very wide variety of uses. Examples include airline seat reservations, police work, and the Prestel information system. These are discussed in chapter 11. One application is described in this chapter, to give you a better idea of how terminals are used.

A POINT-OF-SALE TERMINAL SYSTEM

A large department store has a computer. Amongst other tasks, the computer keeps the accounts of the store, and the stock records.

Instead of an ordinary cash register each cashier has a terminal linked to the computer. These are called **point-of-sale** terminals. For each item sold, a stock number and a price are entered at the terminal. The computer adds up the total for each sale, and sends it to the terminal. If the customer has an account, the amount is charged to that account, otherwise the amount is added to the total cash received. The computer also brings the stock records up to date.

At any time, the computer knows the stock situation in the shop, the amount of cash that has been received and how much is owed by each customer. This information can be used to order stock, send out customer accounts and to balance the cash at the end of each day.

END OF CHAPTER SUMMARY

These are the main points introduced in this chapter:

- Computers often become much more useful when combined with communications networks.

- The hardware devices used to provide direct links with computers are terminals.

- Several computers can be linked together to form a network of computers.

- The range of applications of computers with terminals is very wide.

EXERCISE

1 Answer these questions from the text you have just read.
   a What is a terminal?
   b Name two types of terminal.
   c What is the main advantage of a computer with terminals?
   d List some advantages of networks of computers.
   e What is a point-of-sale terminal?

2 Which of the following activities do you think would be speeded up by using a computer with terminals?
   Military early-warning systems
   Wage calculations
   Keeping stock records at a warehouse
   Producing gas bills

3 Find out (or suggest) some more applications of computers with terminals.

4 Here is another use for a computer with terminals:

A container port has a large container park next to a berth for three container ships. Each container space in the park is numbered. Lorries arrive with containers, and pick up other containers for delivery. Other lorries work within the port, moving containers between the container park and the cranes which load and unload the ships. These lorries are linked by radio to a control room.

The movement of the containers is controlled by a computer. There are terminals at the gate where the lorries arrive and leave, and in the control room.

Think carefully about this system and suggest:

a What information is input at the terminal at the gate when a lorry arrives at the port with a container.

b What information is output at this terminal before the lorry enters the port.

c What information is input and output at the terminals at the control room.

d What information is available from the computer at any time.

CHAPTER 5

HOW A CENTRAL PROCESSING UNIT WORKS

You can see from the photograph below that the central processing unit of a computer is extremely complicated. Yet the essential ideas behind the way a CPU works are quite simple. This chapter introduces these essential ideas, leaving out the details.

You will recall from previous chapters that the CPU is where the various operations of data processing are carried out. A CPU consists of three parts – a memory, an arithmetic and logic unit and a control unit.

In this chapter, a little more detail is given about each part of a CPU. You are introduced to a very simple computer program, and the way in which the CPU carries out the program instructions. In the second part of the chapter, you can learn about the theory behind the workings of a CPU. This theory is called computer logic.

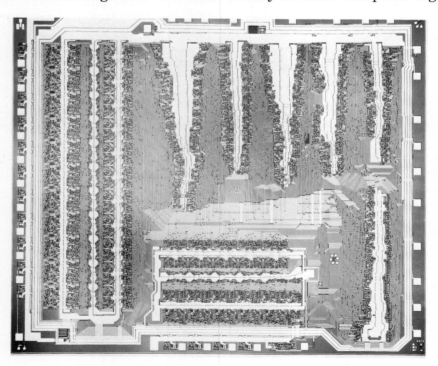

As mentioned in chapter 3, the memory, or main store, of a computer consists of a number of cells. Each cell can store one item of data, or one program instruction.

An essential feature of computer memories is that each cell is numbered. A computer can respond to instructions like: 'Store the letter A in memory cell 97', and 'Fetch the contents of memory cell 51'.

You might also remember that all data and instructions are in code, using the digits 0 and 1 only. However, in this chapter we shall use ordinary numbers and letters, to make things easier.

As you know by now, the arithmetic and logic unit is where program instructions are carried out. Calculations are done and decisions are made by circuits in the ALU.

Just as most people need a piece of paper to jot down numbers when they are doing sums, computers need space to store their working. In the ALU is a space called an **accumulator** where data items can be stored during processing. Many computers have more than one accumulator.

The accumulator can be referred to in program instructions. Thus a computer can carry out an instruction like 'Store the contents of the accumulator in memory cell 84'.

As you will remember, the control unit controls the order in which program instructions are carried out. Most computers can only process one instruction at a time. The control unit 'steers' each instruction through the CPU. It controls the timing of each operation.

When programs are written in a binary code using 0's and 1's only, with one instruction per memory cell, the code is called **machine language**. In the next chapter you will learn that this is not the only way to write computer programs. But machine language instructions are the instructions which a computer processes directly. Machine language is the language in which the computer works. You may be surprised to learn that each machine language instruction carries out a very simple operation. Many computers do not have a machine language instruction for multiplication – it is too complicated! A whole set of machine language instructions is needed for multiplication.

As mentioned previously, machine language instructions can refer to the accumulator, and to any cell in the computer memory.

33

AN EXAMPLE OF A MACHINE LANGUAGE PROGRAM

Below is a very simple example of a program in machine language. It should be written in 0's and 1's only, but short English words and ordinary numbers are used instead, for simplicity. (Strictly speaking, the program is written in a **low-level** language rather than a true machine language.)

The program inputs two numbers and stores them in the computer memory. The numbers are added together, and the total is stored in the memory. The total is also output.

The program is shown as it would appear loaded in the computer memory. Notice how the cells reserved for data are directly after the program.

Cell number	Program instruction	Meaning
1	INP	• Input a number into the accumulator.
2	STO 10	• Store the number in the accumulator in memory cell 10.
3	INP	• Input a number into the accumulator.
4	STO 11	• Store the number in the accumulator in memory cell 11.
5	LOA 10	• Load the number in memory cell 10 into the accumulator.
6	ADD 11	• Add the number in memory cell 11 to the number in the accumulator, and place the sum in the accumulator.
7	STO 12	• Store the number in the accumulator in memory cell 12.
8	OUP	• Output the number in the accumulator.
9	END	• End of program.
10		
11		} Memory cells for data.
12		

The best way of showing how a program works is to run it on a computer. Unfortunately, we cannot do this with the example program. The alternative is to run the program by hand. Each instruction is carried out as it would be on a computer, and the results are written down. This method is called a **dry run**.

Below is a dry run of the example program. You will notice that the program needs two input numbers. For this dry run, the numbers 27 and 41 are chosen.

Next to the program instructions are a number of columns. The first column is for the accumulator, the other columns are for the memory cells used by the program. The numbers written in the columns depend on the program instructions.

Cell No	Instruction	Acc	Cell 10	Cell 11	Cell 12
1	INP	27			
2	STO 10	27	27		
3	INP	41	27		
4	STO 11	41	27	41	
5	LOA 10	27	27	41	
6	ADD 11	68	27	41	
7	STO 12	68	27	41	68
8	OUP	68	27	41	68
9	END	68	27	41	68

Read through the program very carefully. Make sure you can see why each number is placed in each memory cell. Look back at the meanings of the instructions if you are not sure.

Notice that the output from the program is the number 68. This is the sum of the input numbers.

At this stage you might be wondering how computers can do so much when machine language operations are so simple. The answer is that the machine language programs for most tasks are very long. Computers can carry out machine language instructions very, very quickly. In this way, complicated tasks do not take computers too long.

1 Answer these questions from the text you have just read.
 a How is each memory cell in a computer identified?
 b What is an accumulator?
 c How many instructions can most computers carry out at a time?
 d Name two features of a machine language.
 e Do machine language instructions carry out complicated operations?

2 One way of doubling a number is to add it to itself. Below is a low-level language program which inputs a number, stores it in the memory, doubles it and outputs the results.

Cell No.	Instruction	Acc	Cell 6	Meaning
1	INP			
2	STO 6			
3	ADD 6			
4	OUP			
5	END			

 a Copy down the program, and the columns for the dry run.
 b Write down the meaning of each instruction.
 c Dry run the program. Use the number 15 as input data.

3 Here is another low-level language instruction:

SUB 9
Subtract the number in memory cell 9 from the number in the accumulator. Put the answer in the accumulator.
(It can be used with any cell number. 9 is just an example.)
 a Include this instruction in a low-level language program to input two numbers, store them in the memory, subtract them and output the result.
 b Dry run your program, using the input numbers 29 and 15.

4 Using the instructions which have now been introduced, make up low-level language programs of your own. Dry run your programs, using suitable data. Make sure your programs do what you intended them to do.

This section concerns the theory behind the way in which a central processing unit works. It may be left out without causing any problems later.

It has already been mentioned (several times) that both data and instructions are stored inside a computer using the digits 0 and 1 only. Data is processed by combining patterns of 0's and 1's in various ways to produce different patterns.

The operations which computers use to combine 0's and 1's are surprisingly simple, and there are not many of them. These operations are called **logical operations**.

Logical operations can be thought of as **gates**, through which data passes. As the data passes through the gate, the 0's and 1's are combined according to the logical operation.

A logical operation can be described by a table, rather like a multiplication table. This table shows the output for different input combinations of 0 and 1.

The three commonest logical operations are introduced below. They are the **AND**, **OR** and **NOT** operations.

This is the simplest logical operation. It reverses the input, changing a 1 to a 0, or 0 to a 1.

NOT

NOT Table

Input	Output
0	1
1	0

input   output

NOT

NOT gate

AND combines two inputs to produce one output.

AND

AND Table

Input A	Input B	Output
0	0	0
0	1	0
1	0	0
1	1	1

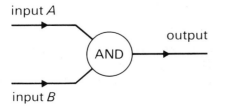

input A

output

AND

input B

AND gate

OR   OR combines two inputs to produce one output.

OR Table

Input A	Input B	Output
0	0	0
0	1	1
1	0	1
1	1	1

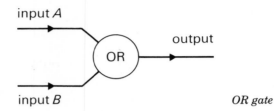

OR gate

The difference between OR and AND can be described like this: AND produces a 1 output if there is a 1 at input A AND at input B. OR produces a 1 output if there is a 1 at input A OR at input B.

COMBINATIONS OF GATES   How can a computer carry out complicated operations if the logical operations it uses are so simple?

The answer is that logic gates are combined. The output from one gate is linked to the input of another gate. In this way, many different kinds of operations can be carried out. Also, if the output from a gate is linked to the input of the same gate, the gate can be used to store data.

A few simple combinations of gates are introduced here, to give you an idea of how they work.

Example 1:
The output of an AND gate is connected to the input of a NOT gate.

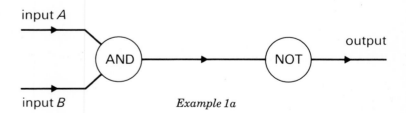

Example 1a

How does it work? To find out, choose a combination of 0's and 1's for the inputs, say input $A = 1$ and input $B = 0$. Then follow this combination through the gates, using the AND table, then the NOT table.

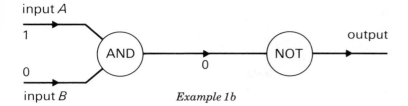

input *A*

1

0

input *B*

AND 0 NOT

output

Example 1b

From the AND table, third row, you can see that the output from the AND gate is 0. The 0 is written next to the output from the AND gate. The 0 is also the input to the NOT gate.

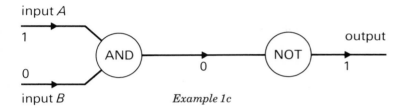

input *A*

1

0

input *B*

AND 0 NOT

output

1

Example 1c

From the NOT table, first row, you can see that the output from the NOT gate is 1. This is the output from the combination of gates when input *A* = 1 and input *B* = 0.

If you try all the other combinations of inputs (there are three of them) you will have enough information to be able to draw up the table for the combination of gates. Here is the table. See if you agree with the results.

Input *A*	Input *B*	Output	
0	0	1	
0	1	1	
1	0	1	• This row comes from the worked example.
1	1	0	

Example 2:
One of the inputs of an OR gate is first passed through a NOT gate.

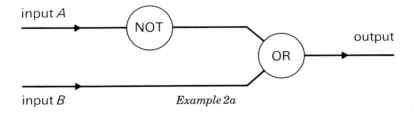

input *A*

NOT OR

output

input *B*

Example 2a

The input combination $A = 0$ and $B = 1$ is followed through the gates in the sketch below.

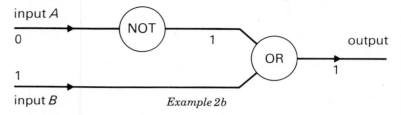

Example 2b

The table below shows the output for all four possible combinations of inputs. Check that you agree with the results.

Input A	Input B	Output	
0	0	1	
0	1	1	• This row comes from the worked example.
1	0	0	
1	1	1	

Most of the combinations of gates used in computers are much more complicated than these examples. Some of the gates have more than two inputs. But the same methods can be used to find out how these combinations of gates work.

END-OF-CHAPTER SUMMARY   Here are the main points of this chapter again:

- Each cell in a computer memory is numbered. It can be referred to by its number.

- The working area used by a computer is called the accumulator.

- Machine language instructions are in a binary code and each one occupies one cell in the memory.

- A machine instruction can refer to the accumulator and to a memory cell by its number.

- One machine instruction carries out one very simple operation.

- Data processing is done by combining patterns of 0's and 1's to produce other patterns of 0's and 1's.

- The basic operations of data processing are called logical operations.

- Logical operations are very simple. They are combined to form more complicated operations.

One important point may have already occurred to you, it is this: The step-by-step operation of a computer is very simple. To perform complicated (and useful) tasks, computers must combine large numbers of simple operations. Some of these combinations are extremely complicated.

1   Answer these questions from the text of this chapter.   **EXERCISE**
    a   What is a logical operation?
    b   What is a gate?
    c   What information is contained in the table of a logical
        operation?
    d   How are logical operations combined?
    e   Are logical operations very complicated?

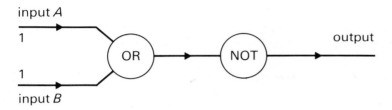

2   a   Follow the inputs $A = 1$ and $B = 1$ through these gates.
    b   Follow other input combinations through the gates.
    c   Draw up a table for this combination of gates.

3   Repeat parts **a**, **b** and **c** of question **2** for each of the following
    combinations of gates. Start with the inputs shown.

a

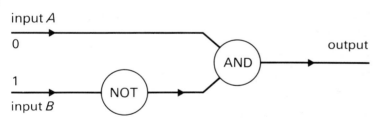

b

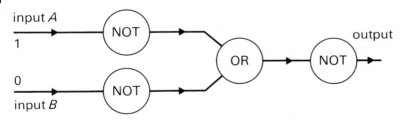

What do you notice about the table for the second combination of
gates?

41

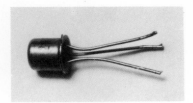

4 In old fashioned computers, each gate was made from one or more **transistors**, like the one shown in the photograph on the left. Look carefully at the photograph below. It shows part of the ALU of an old computer. See how many transistors you can find in the circuit.

CHAPTER 6

KEEPING A COMPUTER RUNNING

The previous chapter gave you some idea of how the central processing unit of a computer works, and how it runs programs. The chapter concentrated on two aspects of a CPU – its hardware and its machine language. You probably realised that the hardware and machine language of a computer on their own do not provide a very useful computer.

This chapter introduces the programs which 'fill the gap' between hardware and a useful computer. These programs keep a computer running. They enable people to use a computer without having to worry about how it works.

SOFTWARE

The bits and pieces which make up a computer are called **hardware**. The programs which keep a computer running are called **software**. Remember:

Hardware + Software = useful computer

There are a number of different types of software, for different purposes. This chapter deals with three types of software: **operating systems**, **user programs**, and **language translation programs**.

OPERATING SYSTEMS

An operating system usually consists of several programs, which work together. These programs are kept on the backing store or in the computer memory all the time. Some, but not all, of the programs are written in machine language.

An operating system has several jobs. The most important jobs are:

● To co-ordinate the various devices which make up the computer. It was mentioned in a previous chapter that these devices work at very different speeds. The operating system tries to make sure that fast devices do not have to wait for slow devices, and that the computer as a whole works efficiently.

● To start up a computer after it has been switched off. Large computers are surprisingly difficult to start up.

- To deal with errors in programs which are running and prevent them spreading to other programs. This is one of the most difficult tasks of an operating system.

- To keep records of the programs run on a computer. The record for each program might include the date and time when it was run, how long it took to run, and its cost.

- To send messages to the person operating the computer, and receive messages from him or her.

As you can imagine, operating systems are extremely complicated. A description of how they work is beyond the scope of this book.

USER PROGRAMS

A user program is a program written by (or for) someone who uses a computer. A user program makes a computer do useful work, like calculating wages, or keeping accounts.

Although the first user programs were written in machine language, this soon proved far too cumbersome. It is not much use having a computer which can do millions of operations per second if it takes months to write programs for it. A number of program languages have been developed to overcome these problems. These languages differ considerably, but have two common features:

- They use English words for instructions, and ordinary maths for calculations.

- They can be used on many different types of computer.

Different languages have been developed for different types of computer applications. There are hundreds of computer languages. A few of the more common ones are mentioned below.

FORTRAN and ALGOL 60 are scientific languages. COBOL, the commonest of them all, is for commercial work. PL/1, ALGOL 68 and PASCAL are general purpose languages. BASIC is a beginner's language, specially designed for use in schools. In the next chapter, you will learn how to write programs in BASIC.

But how is it that computers can only work in machine language, and yet can run programs in all these other languages? As you might have guessed, the answer is – more programs. These are **language translation programs**.

LANGUAGE TRANSLATION PROGRAMS

Language translation programs translate user programs into machine language. Like operating systems, language translation programs are kept on backing store or on the memory of the computer. Language translation programs are sometimes, but not always, written in machine language.

Language translation programs have one other function. If a user program contains an error, it obviously cannot be translated into machine language. The translation program detects errors in user programs, and sends messages to the person who wrote the program. These messages indicate where the error has occurred, and the type of error. The program must be corrected before it can be run. (Notice the difference between this kind of error and the errors detected by an operating system.)

This chapter has given a very brief introduction to the way in which computers are made to perform useful work. Here are the main points again:

- Computers require a number of different kinds of programs to keep them running efficiently.

- Another word for programs is software. Remember:
  hardware + software = useful computer

- Software includes operating systems, user programs and language translation programs.

- A number of different programming languages are now in use, for different purposes.

1 Answer these questions from the text you have just read:
   a   What is software?
   b   Why is software important?
   c   Briefly describe four jobs done by an operating system.
   d   What is a user program?
   e   Name some programming languages.
   f   Name two tasks performed by a language translation program.

2 Here are the names of some more programming languages:
   CORAL, ADA, SIMULA, APL, PL/M.
   a   Find out what these languages are used for.
   b   Find out the names of other programming languages. (There are over 100 in use at present.) Computing magazines are a good source of information.

3 Find out which languages are used by some local computers.

4 Would an operating system or a language translation program do the following tasks:
   a   Decide when to start running a program.
   b   Identify an error in a program when it is running.
   c   Stop a program which is delaying other programs, and re-start it later.
   d   Detect an error in a program while it is being translated.

5 Below is a short program written in ALGOL. It inputs three numbers, adds them up, and outputs the total.

```
begin
      real    a, b, c, t, ;
      read    a, b, c, ;
      t: = a + b + c ;
      print t
end
```

The same program is shown again, written in the low-level language of the previous chapter.

Cell No.	Instruction
1	INP
2	STO 13
3	INP
4	STO 14
5	INP
6	STO 15
7	LOA 13
8	ADD 14
9	ADD 15
10	STO 16
11	OUP
12	END
13	
14	
15	} Memory cells for data
16	

Study the two programs carefully. The second line of the ALGOL program means that the letters **a, b, c,** and **t** are to store (real) numbers. Answer the following questions about the program.

    a Which six instructions from the second program match the **read a, b, c** instructions from the first program?

    b Which memory cell in the second program corresponds to the letter **t** in the first program?

6 You will remember from a previous chapter that data must not be vague. Obviously, computer program instructions cannot be vague either. This is what prevents us from using plain English as a programming language.

Think about the following sentences. See how many meanings you can find for each one:
  a These shoes are guaranteed to give you a fit.
  b We heard about him at school.
  c John's dad is a fat stock breeder.
  d The accused admitted stealing a bicycle and two cases of false pretences.
  e I say that you must not believe anything I say.

CHAPTER 7

HOW TO PROGRAM A COMPUTER

This chapter helps you to put into practice many of the things you have learned about computers. You will learn to write programs of your own. Hopefully you will be able to run your programs on a computer, and see the results. You will also learn how to understand and, if necessary, correct programs written by other people.

Remember that a program is a set of instructions to a computer. The instructions tell the computer how to do a piece of work. When you write a program, you must know how to do the work yourself, even though it might take you a very long time.

BASIC LANGUAGE

In the previous chapter, you learned that there are a number of languages for writing programs. Different program languages are for different purposes. The language introduced here is called BASIC. BASIC stands for Beginners All-purpose Symbolic Instruction Code. It is the most suitable language for you to learn at this stage, for several reasons:

- BASIC resembles ordinary English, and calculations in BASIC resemble ordinary maths.

- BASIC has been designed for use in schools.

- BASIC can be run on many computers, especially small computers built around microprocessors.

You will also remember from the previous chapter that programs in BASIC are translated into machine language before they are run on a computer. However, this is always done for you by the computer. You write a program in BASIC and the computer does the rest.

A **BASIC** PROGRAM

All BASIC programs have a few essential features. It is a good idea to get to know them now:

- Each instruction is written on a new line, starting with a **line number**. When a program is run, the instructions are carried out in order of line number.

- Each instruction has an **instruction word**, which has the same meaning as in ordinary English. The first instruction words you will learn are INPUT, PRINT and END.

- A letter is used for each item of data in a program. These letters are sometimes followed by a $ sign. The letters actually refer to the places in the computer memory where the data items are stored.

Input a person's name and telephone number. Print this information.   **EXAMPLE PROGRAM 1**

The letters chosen for the items of information are:
    N$: name
    T: telephone number
(though any other letters could have been used). Notice that there is a $ sign if the data item is not a number.

Program

```
 5 INPUT N$,T
10 PRINT N$,T
15 END
*
ANDREW EVANS, 246 8091
```

Points to notice:

- Only capital letters are used.

- The line numbers chosen are 5, 10 and 15. Line numbers usually go up in fives so that any lines left out can easily be filled in later.

- The * on a separate line instructs the computer to run the program. On some computers the * is replaced by the word RUN (without a line number).

- After the * is the data needed for the program. Each letter in the INPUT instruction is for one data item. The data must be written in the same order as the letters. In this program, N$ represents ANDREW EVANS and T represents 246 8091.

- If your computer has a visual display unit for output, the results are displayed on a screen, rather than being printed. The word PRINT is still used in the instruction.

Results:

After the program has been run, the results are:

```
ANDREW  EVANS                246  8091
```

EXAMPLE PROGRAM 2

Input the names of three items on sale at a shop, and their prices. Print this information.

The letters chosen for the data are:
  A$, B$, C$ for the names of the items for sale
  P, Q, R for their prices.

Program

```
5 INPUT A$, P, B$, Q, C$, R
10  PRINT A$, P
15  PRINT B$, Q
20  PRINT C$, R
25  END
*
DIGITAL WATCH, 51.95
POCKET CALCULATOR, 6.75
PERSONAL COMPUTER, 499.95
```

Points to notice

- The order of the data corresponds to the order of the letters in the INPUT instruction.

- Each PRINT instruction starts a new line of output, as you can see from the results.

- There are commas between letters in INPUT and PRINT instructions, and between data items on the same line. There are no commas at the ends of lines.

Results

```
DIGITAL WATCH          51.95
POCKET CALCULATOR       6.75
PERSONAL COMPUTER     499.95
```

The program shown below has been written to input the destination, time of departure and time of arrival of two trains, and to print this information.

The letters used are:
D$, E$ for destinations
T, U for departure times
R, S for arrival times

Program

```
5 INPUT D$, T AND R
10 INPUT E$, T, S
15 PRINT D$, T$, R
15 PRINT E$, U, S
25 END.
*
BRISTOL PARKWAY, 1015,1127
EDINBURGH, 1000,1437
```

When this program was run, it was found to contain a number of errors, one in each line, in fact. Below is the same program, with all the errors corrected. See if you can find the errors before looking at the correct program.

Corrected Program

```
5 INPUT D$, T, R
10 INPUT E$, U, S
15 PRINT D$, T, R
20 PRINT E$, U, S
25 END
*
BRISTOL PARKWAY, 1015, 1127
EDINBURGH, 1000, 1437
```

Comments on corrections

- The word AND is replaced by a comma.
- The letter T should have been U.
- The T must not have a $ sign.
- The line number should have been 20.
- There must be no full stop.

- The data is correct.

Results

```
BRISTOL PARKWAY   1015   1127
EDINBURGH         1000   1437
```

A single error in a program can cause it to produce wrong results. In many cases, a program with a single error will not run at all.

Remember: **GARBAGE IN, GARBAGE OUT**

1   Answer these questions from the text you have just read:
   a   What is the first thing on any line of a BASIC program?
   b   What does the   *   at the end of a program tell the computer to do?
   c   What does BASIC stand for?
   d   If a program has one very small error, will it still work correctly?
   e   What is the last instruction in every BASIC program?
   f   What do the letters in a BASIC program do?

2   This program inputs the names and wavelengths of three radio stations, and prints them.

The letters chosen for the data are:
   X$, Y$, Z$ for the names of the stations
   U, V, W   for the wavelengths

Program

```
5 INPUT X$, U, Y$, V, Z$, W
10 PRINT X$, U
15 PRINT Y$, V
20 PRINT Z$, W
25 END
*
CAPITAL RADIO,  194
RADIO 1,        285
RADIO 4,        2500
```

   a   Which data item does   Y$ represent?
   b   How many lines of output are there?
   c   Write down the complete output produced by the program.

3   The program shown on the next page has been written to input and print the names and birthdays of two people.
   Letters: N$, M$ names
                B$, C$ birthdays

Program

```
5 INPUT N$, B$
10 INPUT M$,___
15 PRINT N$___
20 _____
25 _____
*
IAN DURY, 13TH APRIL
```

   a Copy the program and the data, and complete the missing parts.

   b Write down the output produced by the complete program.

4 The following program has been written to input a person's name and address.

   The letters used are:

    N$ name
    A$ first line of address
    B$ second line of address
    C$ third line of address
    P$ postcode

The program written here contains a number of errors (one error in most lines).

Program

```
5 INPUT N$, A$, B$, C$, P$
15 PRINT N$
15 PRINT, A$
20 PRINT B
25 PRINT C$ AND P$
30 THE END
*
```

   a Rewrite the program, correcting all the errors.

   b Supply suitable data for the program.

   c Write down the output produced by the correct program.

5 Write a program to input the names of three football teams, and the points they have scored in their division of the Football League.

    Use the letters **L$**, **M$**, **N$**, for the names, and **P**, **Q** and **R** for the points. Supply your own data.

CALCULATIONS

The programs introduced in the previous section could only input, store and output data. This section introduces calculations in programs.

The BASIC instruction for a calculation contains the word   LET. The calculation is written in a very similar way to ordinary maths.

Some examples of   LET   instructions

5   LET   J = 4

The letter   J   now represents the number   4.

20   LET   C = A + B

This instruction adds together the numbers represented by the letters   A   and   B,   and represents the result by the letter   C.

15   LET   X = 2.5 * Y − Z

In a BASIC calculation, the   *   stands for multiply. This instruction first multiplies the number represented by   Y   by 2.5, and then subtracts the number represented by   Z.   The letter   X   represents the result.

Notice that there must be only one letter before the equals sign in a   LET   instruction.

EXAMPLE PROGRAM 4   Input the distance of a car journey, and the time taken for the journey. Calculate and output the average speed.

Letters: D   distance (miles)
           T   time (hours)
           S   speed (miles per hour)

Speed is calculated by dividing distance by time:
$$S = D \div T$$

Program

```
 5 INPUT D, T
10 LET S=D/T
15 PRINT S
20 END
*
435, 9
```

54

Points to notice

- The symbol / is used for division. To remind you, here are all the BASIC symbols for calculations:

Maths		BASIC
+	stays	+
−	stays	−
×	becomes	*
÷	becomes	/

- There are no units written with the data numbers. Ways of including units are shown later.

Results

```
48.333
```

Input three numbers. Calculate their total, and their average. Output the total and the average.

EXAMPLE PROGRAM 5

Letters used: A, B and C for the input numbers
T   for the total
M   for the average

Calculations: T = A + B + C   add up the numbers to get the total
M = T ÷ 3   divide the total by 3 to get the average

Program

```
5 INPUT A, B, C
10 LET T=A+B+C
15 LET M=T/3
20 PRINT T
25 PRINT M
30 END
*
7, 15, 19
```

Points to notice

- A program can have more than one LET instruction.

- The total is calculated in line 10 and then used in line 15.

Results

```
41
13.6667
```

55

EXAMPLE PROGRAM 6   Input the name of an article, its price and a quantity sold. Work out the cost (cost = price × quantity) and print all the information.

Letters used: **N$**   name of article
              P   price
              Q   quantity
              C   cost

Program

```
5 INPUT N$, P, Q, C
10 LET C=PxQ
15 PRINT N$, P, Q
20 PRINT COST
15 END
*
ELECTRIC DRILL, £19.45, 5
```

This attempt to write the program contains a number of errors. It is written again opposite, with all the errors corrected. See if you can find the errors before looking at the correct program.

A programmer at work

Corrected Program

```
5  INPUT N$, P, Q
10 LET C = P * Q
15 PRINT N$, P, Q
20 PRINT C
25 END
*
ELECTRIC DRILL, 19.45, 5
```

Comments

- The cost C is not input.
- For multiplication.
- No errors.
- Only the letter C must be used for cost.
- Wrong line number.

- No £ sign on the price.

Results

```
ELECTRIC DRILL 19.45   5
97.25
```

1 Write BASIC instructions for these calculations. The first one has been done for you.

BASIC

a $K = M + L$ 10 LET K = M + L   (use any line number)
b $V = M + W$
c $H = 3 \times A - C$
d $J = 2 \times A \div C$
e $W = K \times L - A \times B$
f $X = 3.723 \times J - 2.116 \div B$

2 Each one of these LET instructions contains an error. Rewrite them correctly.

a 5 LET A = B ÷ C
b 35 LET G = A × B − C
c 20 LET A + B + C + D = X
d 30 LET K = 3A + 2B
e 15 LET AREA = LENGTH × BREADTH

3 The following program inputs the carrying capacity (in tonnes) of a type of goods wagon, and the number of these wagons in a train. The carrying capacity of the train is calculated and printed.

Letters used: C capacity of one wagon
                      N number of wagons in the train
                      T capacity of the train.
Calculation: T = C × N

Program

```
 5 INPUT C, __
10 LET T = ____
15 PRINT _____

*
47.5,_____
```

a Copy the program, and complete the missing parts.
b Write down the output that your completed program will produce.

4 The following program inputs the name of an article, and its price. The cash discount is calculated, at a discount rate of 5%. The price less discount is also calculated. The name, price, discount and price less discount are printed.

Letters: R$ name
              P   price
              D   discount
              L   price less discount

Calculations: $D = P \times 5 \div 100$ $(5\% = 5 \div 100)$
$L = P - D$

Program

```
5 INPUT R$, P, D, L
10 LET D=Px5/100
15 LET L=P-D
20 PRINT R$, R, D, L
25 END OF PROGRAM
*
RADIO,   31.30
```

a Rewrite the program, correcting all the errors.
b Write down the output that your corrected program will produce.

Write programs of your own for some of these tasks. Choose your own data.

5 Input the length and breadth of a rectangle, calculate and print its area. Use the letters L and B for length and breadth, and A for area. (Remember $A = L \times B$)

6 Input the speed (mph) of an aeroplane, and a distance which it travels (miles). Calculate the time (hours) which it takes for the journey. Print the speed, distance and time.

Use the letters: S   speed
D   distance
T   time
Calculation: $T = D \div S$

Note on data   Most passenger planes fly at about 600 miles per hour. Concorde does 1500 mph. Some fighter planes can fly even faster. Journey distances vary from 50 to 5000 miles.

7 Input the name of a country, its population and area (square kilometres). Calculate the population density of the country (the number of people per square kilometre).

Use the letters: C$ name of country
P   population
A   area
D   population density
Calculation: $D = P \div A$

Print all the information.

Use a geography textbook or atlas to find suitable data.

MORE PROGRAMS At this stage you may wish to make up programs entirely on your own. A large number of good programs can be written with the BASIC instructions you have learned so far.

Here are some suggestions:

- Programs to do with area or volume
- Programs concerning money: wages, prices, discounts, inflation
- Programs to do with shapes: calculating angles, etc.

More specific suggestions, including some useful formulae, are given at the end of the next exercise.

HEADINGS The appearance of the output of a program is often greatly improved by the use of headings. Headings, units and other information can be printed by using inverted commas in PRINT instructions.

For example, the instruction:

    35 PRINT "TOTAL"

results in the output:

    TOTAL

The instruction:

    50 PRINT "DATE", "AMOUNT", "DISCOUNT"

results in the output:

    DATE   AMOUNT   DISCOUNT

Notice how the commas fit between the inverted commas in line   50.

The instructions:

    25 LET   K = 6.725
    30 PRINT K, "CENTIMETRES"

produce the output:

    6.725   CENTIMETRES

EXAMPLE PROGRAM 7 Input the length, breadth and height of a box and calculate its volume   (volume = length × breadth × height).   Print   all   the information, using suitable headings.

Letters used: L   length
                B   breadth
                H   height
                V   volume

Calculation: $V = L \times B \times H$

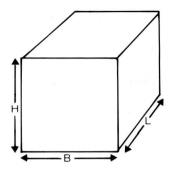

Program

```
 5 INPUT L, B, H
10 LET V=L*B*H
15 PRINT "LENGTH", "BREADTH", "HEIGHT"
20 PRINT L, B, H
25 PRINT "VOLUME"
30 PRINT V
35 END
*
7.5, 18.2, 9.8
```

Points to notice
- Notice how the headings are printed above the items to which they refer.

Results

```
LENGTH              BREADTH             HEIGHT
7.5                 18.2                9.8
VOLUME
1337.7
```

Input a person's name, rate of pay per hour, and number of hours worked in a week. Calculate the person's pay (pay rate × number of hours worked). Print all the information, with suitable headings.

EXAMPLE PROGRAM 8

Letters used: N$ name
               R   rate of pay per hour
               H   hours worked in a week
               P   pay
Calculation: $P = R \times H$

Program

```
5 INPUT N$, R, H
10 LET P=R*H
15 PRINT "NAME", N$
20 PRINT "PAY RATE", R
25 PRINT "HOURS WORKED", H
30 PRINT "PAY", P
35 END
*
A.M. JONES, 3.72, 39
```

Points to notice
- In this program, headings are printed on the same lines as the items to which they refer. Compare this method with the one in the previous example program.

Results

```
NAME            A.M. JONES
PAY RATE        3.72
HOURS WORKED    39
PAY             145.08
```

DRY RUNS

In chapter **5**, programs in a type of machine language were 'run' by writing down the numbers used by each instruction, and doing all calculations by hand.

The same process can be used with BASIC programs. It is called a **dry run**. It is very useful for checking that a program is correct. In most cases, simple data is chosen to make the calculations easy.

A dry run is included in the program which follows.

EXAMPLE PROGRAM 9

Input the fuel consumption (miles per gallon) of a car, and the distance of a journey to be travelled (miles). Calculate the number of gallons required (gallons = distance ÷ miles per gallon). Print all the data, using suitable headings.

Letters: C   fuel consumption
            D   distance
            G   number of gallons

Calculation: $G = D \div C$

Data chosen for dry run: C   30
                           D   600

Program

```
5 INPUT C, D
10 PRINT "FUEL CONSUMPTION", C, "M.P.G."
15 PRINT "DISTANCE", D, "MILES"
20 LET G=D/C
25 PRINT "FUEL REQUIRED", G, "GALLONS"
30 END
*
30, 600
```

C	D	G
30	600	
30	600	
30	600	
30	600	20
30	600	20

Points to notice

• Notice how the units are included in the PRINT instructions. As usual, there are no units in the data numbers.

Results

```
FUEL CONSUMPTION      30    M.P.G.
DISTANCE             600    MILES
FUEL REQUIRED         20    GALLONS
```

END-OF-CHAPTER SUMMARY

• This chapter has introduced the first steps of computer programming in BASIC language.

• The BASIC instruction words INPUT, LET, PRINT and END have been explained. If you think about it, you will realise how these correspond to the ideas of input, processing and output introduced in chapter 1.

• A program in BASIC or any other language, will not run correctly unless it is completely free of errors. One way of checking a program is a dry run, using simple data.

EXERCISE

1 Answer these questions from the text of the whole chapter.
   a What is wrong with the following statement?
   'I don't know how to solve this problem, so I shall get a computer to do it'.
   b What is the difference between the output produced by these two instructions?
   25 PRINT A
   25 PRINT "A"
   c Programs are input in BASIC language. Are they run in BASIC?

d Can the data for a BASIC program be input in any order?

e What is wrong with this section of program?
```
10 LET    C = A + B
15 INPUT A, B
```

2 Write LET instructions for these calculations. The first one has been done for you.

BASIC

a $K = 3 \times M - 4$ 15 LET K = 3 * M − 4

b $T = 5 \times A + 4 \times B$

c $H = A \div B \times C \div D$

d $A = 3.14 \times R \times R$

e $P = 4 \times B + C \times D - 9$

f $G = 1.7162 \times B \times C - 3.9214 \div H$

3 Study the following program and then answer the questions about it.

Program

```
5  INPUT K, L
10 LET J=K−L
15 INPUT M, P
20 LET R=M+P
25 LET T=J*R
30 PRINT "RESULT", T
35 END
*
7, 4
12, 1
```

a What number does M store?

b What is the result of the calculation in line 10?

c Write down the output that would be produced by this program.

4 The next program is designed to estimate the number of litres of paint, both undercoat and top coat, needed to paint a wall. The area of the wall, in square metres, is input. The amount of paint is calculated from the fact that one litre of undercoat covers 6.7 square metres, and one litre of top coat covers 4.8 square metres.

Letters:　　A　area of wall
　　　　　　U　litres of undercoat
　　　　　　T　litres of top coat

Calculations:　U　= A ÷ 6.7
　　　　　　　T　= A ÷ 4.8

Copy the program and complete the missing parts.

Program

```
5  INPUT ___
10 LET U=A/___
15 LET _____
20 PRINT "LITRES  OF  UNDERCOAT", ___
25 PRINT _____
30 ___
*
39.6
```

5 Income tax is (at the time of writing) 30% of a person's taxable income, provided that the income is below a certain limit. Taxable income is gross income less an allowance, which depends on each person's circumstances. Tax is calculated on a yearly basis.

The program below inputs a person's gross income and allowance for a year, and calculates their taxable income and income tax.

Letters used:　G　gross income
　　　　　　　　A　allowance
　　　　　　　　T　taxable income
　　　　　　　　X　tax
Calculations:　$T = G - A$
　　　　　　　　$X = .3 \times T$　　$(30\% = .3)$

a Copy the program and dry run it, using the data in the program.

Program

```
5  INPUT G, A
10 LET T=G-A
15 PRINT "TAXABLE  INCOME",  T
20 LET X=.3*T
25 PRINT "TAX", X
30 END
*
3600, 1200
```

Dry run

G　A　T　X

b Write down the output that this program will produce.

65

6 The following program is to calculate the area of a circle. The radius is input.

Letters: R   radius
                   A   area

Calculation: $A = 3.14 \times R \times R$

Notice the method of 'squaring' the radius in the calculation.

The program, however, contains a number of errors. Rewrite the program, correcting all the errors.

Program

```
 5 INPUT R, A
10  PRINT RADIUS, R
15  LET A=3.14xRxR
20  PRINT AREA
25  END
30*
9.327 CENTIMETRES
```

Questions 7 and 8 Write programs of your own for these tasks. Choose suitable data.

7 The cost of a motorway is £2.7 million per kilometre in open country, and £5.3 million per kilometre through built-up areas. Write a program to input the length of a proposed motorway in open country, and in built-up areas, and calculate the cost of this motorway. Print all the data, using suitable titles and including units.

Suggested letters: P   distance in open country
                        B   distance in built-up areas
                        C   cost (millions of pounds)

Calculation: $C = P \times 2.7 + B \times 5.3$

8 Goods are offered on hire-purchase at the following terms:
A deposit of 20% of the price, twelve equal payments of the remaining amount.

Write a program to input the name and price of an article, and calculate the deposit and amount of each payment. Print all the information, using suitable headings.

Suggested letters: N\$ name of article
                        P   price
                        D   deposit
                        Y   payment

Calculations: D = .2 × P   (20% = .2)
                 Y = (P − D) ÷ 12

Note that brackets may be used in **LET** instructions just as they are in ordinary maths.

SUGGESTIONS FOR MORE PROGRAMS

If you want to make up more programs of your own, you should now have plenty of scope. Here are a few suggestions.

- Example programs can be modified to improve the headings and units. Different data can be used. The same can be done to programs given in exercises.

- More programs can be written concerning area, perimeter or volume. Here are some useful formulae:

Rectangle   Area: $A = L \times B$
Perimeter: $P = 2 \times L + 2 \times B$
L : Length,   B : Breadth

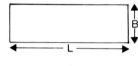

Triangle   Area: $A = B \times H \div 2$
B : Base,   H : Height

Circle   Area: $A = 3.14 \times R \times R$
Circumference: $C = 2 \times 3.14 \times R$
R : Radius

Cylinder   Volume: $V = 3.14 \times R \times R \times H$
R : Radius,   H : Height

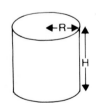

Cone   Volume: $V = 3.14 \div 3 \times R \times R \times H$
R : Radius,   H : Height

Sphere   Volume: $V = 4 \div 3 \times 3.14 \times R \times R \times R$
Surface Area: $A = 4 \times 3.14 \times R \times R$
R : Radius

- More programs can be written about money matters: discount, interest on savings, price increases, inflation.

Here are some useful formulae:

Discount

$D = P \times R \div 100$

$L = P - D$

D : discount

R : discount rate (%)

P : price

L : price less discount

Interest

$I = P \times R \times T \div 100$

I : interest (£)

P : amount saved (£)

R : interest rate (%)

T : time of savings (years)

Price Increases

$I = (N - P) \times 100 \div P$

I : percentage increase

N : new price

P : old price

If N and P are average prices for a number of items measured one year apart, then I estimates the inflation rate.

CHAPTER 8

MORE PROGRAMS TO WRITE

The previous chapter introduced you to computer programming in BASIC. This chapter teaches you a little more about BASIC language, and enables you to write a lot more programs. However, this chapter is not essential to the flow of the whole book. It may be left out if you do not wish to write any more programs.

If you look back at any of the programs in the previous chapter, you will see that they do not do very much. In most cases the tasks can be done just as quickly without using a computer. In this chapter you will learn how to make a computer do much more, using only a few more instructions. You will begin to get some idea of the power of computers.

LOOPS

Like most programming languages, BASIC has instructions which make a computer carry out part of a program repeatedly. A part of a program which is carried out a number of times is called a **loop**. Loops are very useful in getting a lot of work done with only a few instructions.

COUNTERS

When a computer enters a loop, it must be sure of getting out again. The computer must have some way of knowing when it has repeated the loop instructions enough times. In BASIC language, the computer uses a letter to represent the number of times a loop has been repeated. Quite naturally, this letter is called a **counter**.

There are two BASIC instructions to control a loop. One is at the start of the loop, and the other is at the end. The instruction at the start uses the words FOR and TO. The instruction at the end uses the word NEXT. Both instructions refer to the loop counter.

For example, the following instructions repeat a loop five times. The letter   K   is the counter.
    25 FOR K = 1 TO 5
    (instructions to be repeated)
    70 NEXT K

The instructions below repeat a loop twenty times, using the counter X:
    15 FOR X = 1 TO 20
    (instructions to be repeated)
    40 NEXT X
(The line numbers used in these examples are not important. Any suitable line numbers could have been chosen.)

EXERCISE   **1**   These instructions are for a loop which is repeated seven times, using the counter   A.   Complete the missing parts:
    15 FOR A = 1 TO —
    50 NEXT —

Write the instructions which start and end the following loops. Use any suitable line numbers.

2   A loop repeated 20 times, using counter   J.

3   A loop repeated 100 times, using counter   P.

4   A loop repeated   N   times, using counter   C.

5   What is the main advantage of having loops in programs?

PROGRAMS USING LOOPS   A number of example programs are now given. These show various ways in which loops can be used in programs. You will see that the programs remain quite short, but can do much more than previous programs.

EXAMPLE PROGRAM 10   Input the names and lengths of four British rivers and print this data.

Method
The part of the program to be repeated is the input and printing of the data. The letter   A   is the counter. The loop is repeated four times.
Letters: C$ name of river
           P   length (miles)

Program

```
 5 FOR A=1 TO 4
10  INPUT C$, P
15  PRINT C$, P
20  NEXT A
25  END
*
SEVERN,  220
THAMES,  210
TOWY,     68
TAY,     117
```

Points to notice

- There is only one INPUT instruction. Because it is repeated four times, there are four sets of data.

- Each set of data is a river name and its length.

Results

```
SEVERN    220
THAMES    210
TOWY       68
TAY       117
```

Print a table to convert from metres to inches, over distances from 1 metre to 10 metres. Use the fact that 1 metre = 39.4 inches. Print suitable headings.

EXAMPLE PROGRAM 11

Method

First print the headings.

Repeat the next part of the program ten times, using the letter M as loop counter. As M will have the values 1, 2, 3 ... up to 10, it can also represent the number of metres.

The formula to calculate inches (letter I) is
  $I = 39.4 \times M$

In this program (and many others like it), no input instructions are needed, and there is no data.

Program

```
5 PRINT "METRES", "INCHES"
10 FOR M=1 TO 10
15 LET I=39.4*M
20 PRINT M, I
25 NEXT M
30 END
*
```

Points to notice

- Notice how the loop counter **M** is also used both in the calculation and printing instructions. This is a very useful feature of loop counters.

- Notice how short the program is for the amount of work it does.

Results

METRES	INCHES
1	39.4
2	78.8
3	118.2
4	157.6
5	197.0
6	236.4
7	275.8
8	315.2
9	354.6
10	394.0

EXAMPLE PROGRAM 12   The area of a triangle is calculated from the length of its base and its height. Write a program to input the base and height of each of three triangles. Calculate the area of each triangle. The formula is:
area = ½ × base × height.

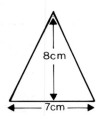

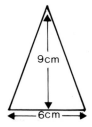

Print a table of length, height and area.

Method

The headings are printed first. The next part of the program is repeated three times, using loop counter N.

Inside the loop, the base (letter B) and height (letter H) are input. The area (letter A) is calculated, using the formula:
$$A = B \times H \div 2$$

The base, height and area are printed, and the loop continues.

Program

```
 5 PRINT "BASE", "HEIGHT", "AREA"
10 FOR N=1 TO 3
15 INPUT B, H
20 LET A=B*H/2
25 PRINT B, H, A
30 NEXT N
35 END
*
7, 8
5, 4
6, 9
```

Points to notice

- Notice how the headings are printed before the loop starts.

- Inside the loop, there is an input, a processing and an output operation. This is a very common pattern.

Results

BASE	HEIGHT	AREA
7	8	28
5	4	10
6	9	27

DRY RUNS

As mentioned in previous chapters, a dry run is a very good way of checking that a program is correct. When dry running programs with loops, the dry run is repeated the same number of times as the loop is repeated.

Below is a dry run of the program from example **12**. Note that part of the dry run is repeated three times.

Program

```
5 PRINT "BASE", "HEIGHT", "AREA"
10 FOR N=1 TO 3
15 INPUT B, H
20 LET A=B*H/2
25 PRINT B, H, A
30 NEXT N
35 END
*
7, 8
5, 4
6, 9
```

Dry run

First time around loop				Second time around loop				Third time around loop			
N	B	H	A	N	B	H	A	N	B	H	A
1				2	7	8	28	3	5	4	10
1	7	8		2	5	4	28	3	6	9	10
1	7	8	28	2	5	4	10	3	6	9	27
1	7	8	28	2	5	4	10	3	6	9	27
2	7	8	28	3	5	4	10				

You might ask 'Why dry run a program, when all the work will be done on a computer when the program is run?' Remember that a dry run is for checking purposes. A dry run will almost always show up errors in a program. Although a dry run of a complicated program takes a long time, it is usually worth the effort.

Also remember that once a program is correct, it can be used again and again, with different data.

EXERCISE

1 Answer these questions from the text of the chapter so far.
   a What is a loop?
   b What is a counter?
   c Why does a computer need a loop counter?
   d Can a loop counter be used for any other purposes?
   e Why is it sometimes useful to dry run a BASIC program?

2 The following program inputs the names and prices of three articles, and prints the information. It is program example **2**, from the previous chapter, done by a different method.

Letters: N$ name of article
          P   price
          J   counter (1 to 3)

Program

```
5 FOR J=1 TO 3
10  INPUT N$, P
15  PRINT N$, P
20  NEXT J
25  END
*
DIGITAL WATCH, 31.95
POCKET CALCULATOR, 6.75
PERSONAL COMPUTER, 499.95
```

Look carefully at the program, and then answer these questions:
a   What information does   N$ represent, the first time around the loop?
b   What number does   P   represent, the second time around the loop?
c   Why are there three lines of input data, but only one   INPUT   instruction?

3   The program below is to convert inches to centimetres, over the range 1 inch to 12 inches. (1 inch = 2.54 centimetres).

Letters: I   inches and loop counter
             C   centimetres
Formula: $C = 2.54 \times I$

a   Copy the program and complete the missing parts.

Program

```
5  PRINT "INCHES," _____
10  FOR I=1 TO ____
15  LET C= _____
20  PRINT ___ , ___
25  NEXT ___
30  END
*
```

b   Write down the first three lines of output your program will produce.
c   If the program is modified to repeat the loop twenty times, which number must be altered?

4 The following program is a different kind of conversion program from ones you have met so far. The program inputs four weights in pounds and converts them to grams (1 pound = 453 grams).

Letters: K   loop counter (1 to 4)
               L   pounds
               G grams
Formula: $G = 453 \times L$

Copy the program and dry run it.

Program

```
5  PRINT "POUNDS",  "GRAMS"
10 FOR K=1 TO 4
15 INPUT L
20 LET G=453*L
25 PRINT L, G
30 NEXT K
35 END
*
2, 10, 5, 4
```

5 Write a program to print a conversion table from pounds to dollars. When this book was written, the conversion rate was £1.00 = $2.40, but the rate is changing all the time. Use an up-to-date figure.

Your program must print suitable headings, and cover the range £1 to £20.

Suggested letters: P pounds and loop counter
                         D dollars
Formula: $D = 2.40 \times P$ (change the 2.40 to an up-to-date figure)

Australia $	2.09
Austria Sch	33.50
Belgium Fr	76.25
Canada $	2.90
Denmark Kr	14.45
Finland Mkk	9.43
France Fr	10.80
Germany DM	4.70
Greece Dr	120.00
Hongkong $	12.45
Ireland Pd	1.24
Italy Lir	2230.00
Japan Yn	532.00
Netherlands Gld	5.08
Norway Kr	12.37
Portugal Esc	128.00
South Africa Rd	1.94
Spain Pta	184.50
Sweden Kr	10.60
Switzerland Fr	4.23
USA $	2.46
Yugoslavia Dnr	82.00

6 Write a program to convert from pounds to one of the foreign currencies in the table on the left. (The table shows how much of each currency you could buy for £1.)

76

You should now be able to write quite a wide variety of programs. Here are some suggestions:

- Conversion tables to other foreign currencies. Look up the conversion rates in a newspaper, or ask at a bank. One program can convert from pounds to several foreign currencies in one loop.

- Many of the programs suggested at the end of chapter **7** can be extended to perform the calulation repeatedly, using several sets of data.

- The example programs in this chapter can be modified to process more data.

A single instruction like:

ADDING UP TOTALS IN LOOPS

15 LET   T = A + B + C

can be used to add up three numbers. But what about twenty numbers, or a thousand numbers? This method will not work.

A program loop can be used to add up to a large number of numbers. The method is quite simple:

- Before the loop starts, set the total to zero.

- Inside the loop, add a number to the total. Repeat the loop once for each number to be added.

- After the loop you will have the total of all the numbers.

Using the letters   T   for the total and   N   for a number, the two BASIC instructions needed are:

Before the loop: 15 LET   T = 0
Inside the loop: 35 LET   T = T + N

At first, the instruction inside the loop looks rather odd, with the letter   T   appearing twice. The instruction changes the total by adding on another number.

The next few program examples show this method of adding totals. When you look at the programs, notice carefully what is done before the loop, what is done inside the loop and what is done after the loop.

Input six numbers and add them up. Print the numbers and their total.

EXAMPLE PROGRAM 13

Method
The method just explained of adding up totals in loops is used. Only three letters are needed: N   for a number,   T   for the total and   X   for the loop counter (from 1 to 6).

Program

```
 5 PRINT "NUMBERS"
10 LET T=0
15 FOR X=1 TO 6
20 INPUT N
25 LET T=T+N
30 PRINT N
35 NEXT X
40 PRINT "TOTAL", T
45 END
*
7, 11, 17, 19, 31, 8
```

Points to notice
- Inside the loop there is an input, a processing and an output operation.

- The numbers are printed inside the loop, but the total is printed outside the loop.

Results

```
NUMBERS
  7
 11
 17
 19
 31
  8
TOTAL                    93
```

EXAMPLE PROGRAM 14   The weekly transport costs of a company are made up of the following items: drivers' wages, petrol costs, insurance and maintenance costs. Write a program to input each item name and the amount spent on it. Calculate the total cost. Print all the data, together with the total. Use suitable headings.

Method
The method of adding up the total is the same as before.

Letters: N$ item name
          C   cost
          T   total cost
          W   counter

Program

```
5  PRINT "ITEM", "COST"
10 LET T=0
15 FOR W=1 TO 4
20 INPUT N$, C
25 LET T=T+C
30 PRINT N$, C
35 NEXT W
40 PRINT "TOTAL", T
45 END
*
DRIVERS WAGES,           517.50
PETROL COSTS,            180.09
INSURANCE,                30.50
MAINTENANCE COSTS,        43.37
```

Results

```
ITEM                 COST
DRIVERS WAGES        517.50
PETROL COSTS         180.09
INSURANCE             30.50
MAINTENANCE COST      43.37
TOTAL                721.46
```

Input the length and breadth of four rooms to be carpeted. Calculate the area of each room, and the total area. Calculate the cost of all the carpeting required, at £5.95 per square metre. Print the length, breadth and area of each room, the total area and the cost of the carpet.

EXAMPLE PROGRAM 15

Method
There is a lot to do in this program!

Before the loop, the headings are printed and the total set to zero. Inside the loop, the length and breadth of a room are input. The area is calculated, and added to the total. The length, breadth and area of the room are printed.

After the loop, the cost is calculated. The total area and the cost are printed.

Letters: L, B length and breadth of a room (metres)
          A   area of a room (square metres)
          T   total area (square metres)
          C   cost (£)
          N   loop counter (from 1 to 4)
Formula: $C = 5.95 \times T$

Program

```
 5 PRINT "LENGTH", "BREADTH", "AREA"
10 LET T=0
15 FOR N=1 TO 4
20 INPUT L, B
25 LET A=L*B
30 LET T=T+A
35 PRINT L, B, A
40 NEXT N
45 LET C=5.95*T
50 PRINT "TOTAL AREA", T
55 PRINT "COST", C
60 END
*
5.4, 5.2
2.7, 3.5
6.8, 4.9
2.1, 2.4
```

Points to notice
- The area of a room is calculated before it is added to the total.

Results

LENGTH	BREADTH	AREA
5.4	3.2	17.28
2.7	3.5	9.45
6.8	4.9	33.32
2.1	2.4	5.04
TOTAL AREA		65.09
COST	387.28	

1 Answer these questions from the text you have just read.
   a Why is it impossible to add up very many numbers in a single program instruction?
   b Describe the two steps needed to add up a total using a loop.
   c Can a total be printed inside the loop in which it is being added up?

2 The program below inputs ten numbers, adds them up, and prints the total. The letter   T   is used for the total, and   X   is used for a number.   K   is the loop counter.

Program

```
5 LET T=
10 FOR K=1 TO
15 INPUT
20 LET T=
25 NEXT
30 PRINT
35 END
*
7, 9, 8, 15, 23
8, 14, 5, 6, 11
```

   a Copy the program and fill in the missing parts.
   b What output is produced by the program?

3 The program below calculates the sum of the squares of the numbers from 1 to 4. (The square of a number is the number multiplied by itself.) The program has no input data. The loop counter is used as the number to be squared.

   Letters: N loop counter and number
             S square of number
             T sum of squares
   Formula: $S = N \times N$

Program

```
5 LET T=0
10 FOR N=1 TO 4
15 LET S=N*N
20 LET T=T+S
25 NEXT N
30 PRINT "SUM OF SQUARES", T
35 END
*
```

a Copy the program and dry run it.

b Which number must be changed for the program to calculate the sum of the square of the first 20 numbers?

4 Write a program to work out telephone call charges. For each call, the time, (in minutes) and the cost per minute (in pence) are input. The cost of the call is calculated. This is done for five calls, and the total cost is added up.

Letters: M time of a call
           P cost per minute
           C cost of a call
           T total cost.
Formula: $C = M \times P$

Use a telephone call charges book to work out the cost per minute of different types of telephone calls. The cost per minute depends on the distance and the time of day.

5 An aeroplane carries first class, business class and tourist class passengers. On a particular flight there are 39, 89, and 146 passengers in the three classes respectively. The first class fare is £285, the business class fare is £195 and the tourist class fare is £145. Use this data in a program to calculate the total amount paid by all the passengers on the flight.

Choose your own letters, and work out the formula which you will need.

6 Write a program to input twenty numbers, and calculate and print their average.

7 The program below calculates the number of hours a person has worked in a week. The person's clocking-on and clocking-off times are the input data. To keep the program simple, only hours (using the 24 hour clock) are input. For example:

Clocking-on time 0900 hours, input data 09
Clocking-off time 1700 hours, input data 17

The hours worked in a day are calculated by subtracting the clocking-on time from the clocking-off time. The total hours for a five day week is calculated.

Letters: N clocking-on time
           F clocking-off time
           H hours worked in a day
           T total hours worked in a week
           L loop counter (from 1 to 5)
Formula: $H = F - N$

a The program contains a number of errors. Rewrite the program, correcting all these errors.

Program

```
 5 LET T=0
10 INPUT N, F
15 FOR L=1 TO 5
20 LET H=N-F
25 LET T+H=T
30 NEXT T
35 PRINT "TOTAL HOURS", T
40 END
```

b Modify the program to print the following headings, with the appropriate data underneath.
TIME ON   TIME OFF   HOURS WORKED

c Supply a suitable set of data for the program.

d Extend the program to input the person's wage rate (money earned per hour) and calculate their weekly wage. Use the letters R for the wage rate and W for the wage. The formula you need is

$W = R \times T$

where T is the total hours from the previous part of the program.

CHAPTER 9

PACKAGES

A **package** is a computer program, or set of programs, which are 'all wrapped up and ready to use'. Many different kinds of packages are available. Some packages control the way in which a computer is put to work. Other packages are for doing certain tasks on a computer.

Most packages are designed to be used by people who are not skilled computer programmers. The people using the package must know what the package does, but they do not need to know any details about how the package works.

This chapter introduces a number of packages. Each package covers a specific activity. The intention of the chapter is to teach you how to work with a computer program. You will learn to use a computer as a tool to solve a problem.

You do not need to know how the programs work, although they are there for you to see. Each package contains instructions on how to use it. When you use a package, all you need to do is follow the instructions.

HOW TO USE THE PACKAGES First read the introduction to the package from this book. It is not necessary to read the program description, unless you want to change the program.

Then load the program onto your computer, or call it up if it is already loaded. If you have to type the program in, do so very carefully. Check the program thoroughly before you try to run it. Remember that a single mistake will almost certainly cause the program to fail.

Start the program running, and read the instructions that are displayed or printed. Then work through the program, supplying input data when it is requested.

This package is designed to improve your ability to spell.

You are presented with a number of words, each of which is wrongly spelt. You are given three attempts to spell the word correctly.

A score is kept. You get 3 points for a correct first attempt, 2 points for a correct second attempt, 1 point for a correct third attempt.

This is a very brief description of the working of the program. It is only necessary to read it if you want to modify the program.

PROGRAM OUTLINE

1	(lines 200–250)	Display instructions for the use of the program.
2	(lines 300–465)	Read list of words and 'shuffle' it according to a random number (today's lucky number) which has been input.
3	(lines 470–480)	Set the score to zero.
4	(lines 500–570)	Each turn: **4.1** Display next mis-spelt word. **4.2** Input attempt to spell the word correctly. **4.3** If the attempt is correct, update the score and go to step **5**. **4.4** If the attempt is wrong, give another chance, go to step **4.2**. **4.5** If no more attempts are allowed, display the correct spelling.
5	(lines 575–655)	Display the score, ask if another word is wanted. If so, go to step **4**.

Important note
This program uses the   RND   function to generate random numbers. Unfortunately this function works slightly differently on different computers. Lines   060   and   105   of this program may have to be altered.

Program

```
100 REM INTRODUCING COMPUTERS: PACKAGE 1
105 REM SPELLING TESTER
110 REM WRITTEN BY P.J.BISHOP ON 22/12/79
115 REM
120 DIM C$(100),W$(100)
125 REM
200 REM DISPLAY INITIAL USER INSTRUCTIONS
```

Cont ...

```
205  PRINT " THIS PACKAGE IS DESIGNED TO"
210  PRINT " IMPROVE YOUR ABILITY TO SPELL."
215  PRINT " YOU ARE PRESENTED WITH A NUMBER OF"
220  PRINT " WORDS, EACH OF WHICH IS SPELLED"
225  PRINT " WRONGLY. YOU HAVE THREE ATTEMPTS"
230  PRINT " TO SPELL THE WORD CORRECTLY."
235  PRINT " TO START THE PROGRAM, PLEASE TYPE"
240  PRINT " IN YOUR LUCKY NUMBER FOR TODAY."
245  PRINT
250  REM
300  REM INPUT RANDOM NUMBER INITIALISER
305  INPUT X
310  REM INITIALISE RANDOM NUMBER GENERATOR
315  REM MAY HAVE TO BE CHANGED TO SUIT
320  REM DIFFERENT COMPUTERS
325  LET X=RND(-X)
330  REM
335  REM READ LIST OF WORDS
340  FOR J=1 TO 101
345  READ W1$,C1$
350  IF C1$="XXX" THEN 400
355  LET C$(J)=C1$
360  LET W$(J)=W1$
365  NEXT J
370  REM
400  REM SHUFFLE LIST OF WORDS
405  FOR I=1 TO J-1
410  REM SELECT NEXT RANDOM NUMBER IN SEQUENCE
415  REM MAY HAVE TO BE CHANGED TO SUIT
420  REM DIFFERENT COMPUTERS
425  LET X=INT(RND(1)*(J-1))+1
430  LET T$=C$(X)
435  LET U$=W$(X)
440  LET C$(X)=C$(I)
445  LET W$(X)=W$(I)
450  LET C$(I)=T$
455  LET W$(I)=U$
460  NEXT I
465  REM
470  REM INITIALISE SCORE
475  LET S=0
480  REM
500  REM START OF A TURN
505  FOR K=1 TO J-1
510  PRINT " TRY TO SPELL  ";W$(K);"  CORRECTLY"
515  PRINT
520  REM INPUT ATTEMPTS AT CORRECT SPELLING
```

```
525 FOR Y=3 TO 1 STEP -1
530 INPUT Z$
535 IF Z$=C$(K) THEN 565
540 PRINT " WRONG"
545 NEXT Y
550 PRINT
555 PRINT "BAD LUCK. THE CORRECT SPELLING IS ";
557 PRINT C$(K)
560 GOTO 585
565 PRINT " WELL DONE. THAT IS CORRECT."
570 PRINT
575 REM UPDATE SCORE
580 LET S=S+Y
585 PRINT "YOUR SCORE IS ";S;" OUT OF ";3*K
590 PRINT
595 PRINT " DO YOU WANT TO TRY ANOTHER WORD?"
597 PRINT " TYPE YES OR NO"
600 PRINT
605 INPUT R$
610 IF R$="YES" THEN 620
615 GOTO 645
620 NEXT K
625 PRINT " SORRY, BUT THERE ARE NO MORE WORDS"
630 PRINT
635 PRINT " YOUR FINAL SCORE IS ";S;" OUT OF ";
637 PRINT 3*(K-1)
640 STOP
645 PRINT
650 PRINT " YOUR FINAL SCORE IS ";S;" OUT OF ";
652 PRINT 3*K
655 STOP
660 REM
700 REM LIST OF WORDS, IN ORDER WRONG SPELLING,
705 REM CORRECT SPELLING, ETC.
710 REM MAXIMUM LENGTH 100 WORDS
715 REM
720 DATA "LISENSE","LICENCE"
725 DATA "PROCEEDURE","PROCEDURE"
730 DATA "JOURNY","JOURNEY"
735 DATA "INDEPENDANT","INDEPENDENT"
740 DATA "EXISTANCE","EXISTENCE"
745 DATA "SOMONE","SOMEONE"
750 DATA "CHARCTER","CHARACTER"
755 DATA "USAL","USUAL"
760 DATA "DIFFRENT","DIFFERENT"
765 DATA "GOVERMENT","GOVERNMENT"
770 DATA "DISSCUSS","DISCUSS"
```

Cont ...

```
775 DATA "ARGUEMENT","ARGUMENT"
780 DATA "DANGROUS","DANGEROUS"
785 DATA "SENSABLE","SENSIBLE"
790 DATA "INCREDABLE","INCREDIBLE"
795 DATA "RESISTENCE","RESISTANCE"
800 DATA "MESAGE","MESSAGE"
805 DATA "SUFFERRED","SUFFERED"
810 DATA "PROBLY","PROBABLY"
815 DATA "QESTION","QUESTION"
985 DATA "XXX","XXX"
990 REM NOTE END-OF-DATA MARKER
995 END
```

PACKAGE 2
ENGLISH-FRENCH
TRANSLATOR

This package translates English words into French, or French words into English. All you have to do is type the word to be translated. The computer will display the translated word.

PROGRAM OUTLINE

1	(lines 200–235)	Display instructions for the use of the program.
2	(lines 300–330)	Load the list of words which the program can translate.
3	(lines 400–460)	Request the type of translation to be performed: 1 for English to French, 2 for French to English.
4	(lines 500–525)	Input the word to be translated.
5	(lines 530–575)	Look for the word in the list. If it is found, display the translation, if not, apologise.
6	(lines 600–635)	Ask whether there are any more words to be translated. If so, go to step 3.

Program

```
100 REM INTRODUCING COMPUTERS: PACKAGE 2
105 REM ENGLISH/FRENCH TRANSLATOR
110 REM WRITTEN BY P.J.BISHOP ON 22/12/79
115 REM
120 DIM W$(101,2)
125 REM
200 REM DISPLAY INITIAL USER INSTRUCTIONS
```

```
205   PRINT " THIS PROGRAM TRANSLATES ENGLISH"
210   PRINT " WORDS INTO FRENCH, OR FRENCH WORDS"
215   PRINT " INTO ENGLISH. YOU TYPE THE WORD TO"
220   PRINT " BE TRANSLATED, AND THE COMPUTER"
225   PRINT " WILL DISPLAY THE TRANSLATED WORD."
230   PRINT
235   REM
300   REM LOAD LIST OF ENGLISH AND FRENCH WORDS
305   REM
310   FOR I=1 TO 101
315   READ W$(I,1),W$(I,2)
320   IF W$(I,1)="***" THEN 405
325   NEXT I
330   REM
400   REM REQUEST TYPE OF TRANSLATION WANTED
405   PRINT " DO YOU WANT TO TRANSLATE FROM"
410   PRINT " ENGLISH TO FRENCH OR FROM FRENCH"
415   PRINT " TO ENGLISH? TYPE 1 FOR ENGLISH TO"
420   PRINT " FRENCH OR 2 FOR FRENCH TO ENGLISH"
425   PRINT
430   REM
435   INPUT T
440   IF T=1 THEN 505
445   IF T=2 THEN 515
450   PRINT " PLEASE TYPE 1 OR 2"
455   GOTO 425
460   REM
500   REM INPUT WORD TO BE TRANSLATED
505   PRINT " TYPE ENGLISH WORD"
510   GOTO 520
515   PRINT " TYPE FRENCH WORD"
520   INPUT X$
525   REM
530   REM LOOK UP WORD IN LIST
535   FOR J=1 TO I-1
540   IF X$=W$(J,T) THEN 565
545   NEXT J
550   PRINT " SORRY, BUT THE WORD ";X$;
555   PRINT " IS NOT IN THE LIST"
560   GOTO 570
565   PRINT X$;" TRANSLATES TO ";W$(J,3-T)
570   PRINT
575   REM
600   PRINT " DO YOU WANT TO TRANSLATE ANY MORE"
605   PRINT " WORDS? TYPE YES OR NO"
610   INPUT R$
```

Cont...

```
615 IF R$="YES" THEN 405
620 PRINT
625 PRINT "END OF PROGRAM REACHED"
630 PRINT
635 STOP
700 REM DATA IS IN ORDER ENGLISH, FRENCH,
705 REM ENGLISH, FRENCH, ETC.
710 REM MAXIMUM LENGTH 100 WORDS
715 REM
720 DATA "AFTER","APRES"
725 DATA "AGAIN","ENCORE"
730 DATA "BEFORE","AVANT"
735 DATA "BETWEEN","ENTRE"
740 DATA "BIG","GRAND"
745 DATA "COLD","FROID"
750 DATA "DRINK","BOIRE"
755 DATA "EAT","MANGER"
760 DATA "EARTH","TERRE"
765 DATA "ENOUGH","ASSEZ"
770 DATA "EVERYTHING","TOUT"
775 DATA "FAST","VITE"
780 DATA "GOOD","BON"
785 DATA "HERE","ICI"
790 DATA "HIGH","HAUT"
795 DATA "HOW","COMMENT"
800 DATA "IN","DANS"
805 DATA "LESS","MOINS"
810 DATA "LITTLE","PETIT"
815 DATA "MORE","PLUS"
820 DATA "NO","NON"
825 DATA "OPEN","OUVERT"
830 DATA "UNDER","SOUS"
835 DATA "VERY","TRES"
840 DATA "WITHOUT","SANS"
845 DATA "YES","OUI"
985 DATA "***","***"
990 REM NOTE END-OF-DATA MARKER
995 END
```

This package helps you to estimate the number of rolls of wallpaper you will need to wallpaper a room, or a house. You will need to supply the following information:

- The number of walls to be papered
- The length and height (in metres) of each wall
- The number of doors and/or windows in the walls
- The length and height of each door and window

1	(lines 200–245)	Display instructions for the use of the program.
2	(lines 300–325)	Input the number of walls to be covered.
3	(lines 330–365)	Input length and height (metres) of each room.
4	(lines 370–382)	Input the number of doors, and/or windows.
5	(lines 385–430)	Input length and height (metres) of each door and window.
6	(lines 360 and 415)	Calculate the wall area to be covered. If this area is negative, output a suitable message and go to step 2.
7	(lines 500–510)	Calculate number of rolls of wallpaper needed. (Allow for 10% wastage, and round up to the next roll.)
8	(lines 515–625)	Output results.
9	(lines 700–735)	Ask if the program is needed again. If so, go to step 2.

Program

```
100 REM INTRODUCING COMPUTERS: PACKAGE 3
105 REM WALLPAPER ESTIMATOR
110 REM WRITTEN BY P.J.BISHOP ON 22/12/79
115 REM
200 REM DISPLAY USER INSTRUCTIONS
205 PRINT " THIS PACKAGE HELPS YOU TO"
210 PRINT " ESTIMATE THE NUMBER OF ROLLS OF"
215 PRINT " WALLPAPER YOU WILL NEED TO"
220 PRINT " WALLPAPER A ROOM, OR A HOUSE. YOU"
225 PRINT " WILL NEED TO SUPPLY VARIOUS ITEMS"
230 PRINT " OF INFORMATION. TYPE THESE IN AS"
235 PRINT " THEY ARE REQUESTED"
240 PRINT
245 REM
300 REM INPUT MEASUREMENTS OF WALLS, DOORS AND
305 REM WINDOWS
310 PRINT " TYPE THE NUMBER OF WALLS"
315 PRINT " TO BE COVERED"
320 PRINT
325 INPUT N
330 PRINT " TYPE THE LENGTH AND HEIGHT"
335 PRINT " (IN METRES) OF EACH WALL"
340 LET A=0
345 FOR K=1 TO N
350 INPUT L,H
355 REM CALCULATE TOTAL WALL AREA
360 LET A=A+L*H
365 NEXT K
370 PRINT " TYPE THE NUMBER OF DOORS"
375 PRINT " AND WINDOWS IN THESE WALLS"
380 INPUT M
382 IF M=0 THEN 425
385 PRINT " TYPE THE LENGTH AND HEIGHT (IN"
390 PRINT " METRES) OF EACH DOOR AND WINDOW"
395 REM
400 FOR J=1 TO M
405 INPUT L,H
410 REM REDUCE WALL AREA BY DOOR OR WINDOW AREA
415 LET A=A-L*H
420 NEXT J
425 IF A<0 THEN 600
430 REM
500 REM CALCULATE NUMBER OF ROLLS OF WALLPAPER
```

```
505 LET R=INT(A/5.0*1.1+1)
510 REM
515 REM OUTPUT RESULTS
520 PRINT
525 PRINT " TOTAL AREA TO BE COVERED: ";A;
530 PRINT " SQUARE METRES"
535 PRINT
540 PRINT " NUMBER OF ROLLS OF WALLPAPER";
545 PRINT " NEEDED: ";R
550 PRINT
555 GOTO 700
560 REM
600 PRINT " YOUR FIGURES ARE WRONG SOMEWHERE,"
605 PRINT " THE WALL AREA IS NEGATIVE."
610 PRINT " PLEASE START AGAIN"
615 PRINT
620 GOTO 310
625 REM
700 PRINT " DO YOU WANT TO USE THE WALLPAPER"
705 PRINT " ESTIMATOR AGAIN? TYPE YES OR NO"
710 INPUT R$
715 IF R$="YES" THEN 310
720 PRINT
725 PRINT " END OF PROGRAM REACHED"
730 PRINT
735 END
```

Use the wallpaper estimator package to answer these questions.   **EXERCISE**
Calculate the number of rolls of wallpaper needed for:

1 One wall, 3.1 m by 2.8 m, no doors or windows
2 Three walls, 2.1 m by 2.6 m, 4.0 m by 2.6 m and 3.0 m by 2.6 m, no
   doors or windows
3 Two walls, 3.8 m by 3.0 m, 4.2 m by 3.0 m with a window 1.5 m by
   2.1 m and a door 1.0 m by 2.2 m
4 Four walls, two 3.2 m by 3.5 m and two 4.6 m by 3.5 m. One door
   1.1 m by 2.3 m, one window 2.0 m by 1.8 m.
5 Other walls with your own measurements.

When you save money at the Post Office, or at a building society, or with some types of bank account, you are paid interest on your money. The interest is a certain percentage of the money you have saved. It is usually paid once or twice a year.

You may wish to save a single amount, or a regular amount at monthly or weekly intervals. This package helps you plan your savings. It tells you how much you will have saved after a certain period of time.

PROGRAM OUTLINE	**1** (lines **200–250**)	Display instructions for the use of the program.
	2.1	Display first question: What kind of savings do you have in mind?
	2.2	Input answer.
	2.3 (lines **300–360**)	Check answer.
	3–7	As for step **2**, with the questions: How much money do you want to save? For how long do you want to save? What interest rate will you get? How often is the interest paid?
	(lines **400–850**)	What kind of report do you want?
	8 (lines **900–1115**)	Calculate the amount saved and print the report. If a single amount is saved, the ordinary compound interest formula is used. If a regular amount is saved, the contribution to the interest from each payment is calculated, using an arithmetic progression. The interest is added to the amount saved at the end of each year or half-year, and at the end of the period of saving.
	9 (lines **1120–1160**)	Find out if the savings planner is required again. If so, go to step **2.1**

Program

```
100  REM INTRODUCING COMPUTERS: PACKAGE 4
105  REM MONEY SAVINGS PLANNER
110  REM WRITTEN BY P.J. BISHOP
115  REM
200  PRINT " THIS PACKAGE HELPS YOU PLAN YOUR"
205  PRINT " SAVINGS. IT TELLS YOU HOW MUCH YOU"
210  PRINT " WILL HAVE SAVED AFTER A CERTAIN"
215  PRINT " PERIOD OF TIME."
220  PRINT " TO USE THE PACKAGE, ANSWER THE"
225  PRINT " QUESTIONS AS THEY ARE DISPLAYED."
230  PRINT " IF YOU WANT TO STOP THE PROGRAM AT"
235  PRINT " ANY STAGE, TYPE 0 IN REPLY TO THE"
240  PRINT " NEXT QUESTION"
245  PRINT
250  REM
300  PRINT " WHAT KIND OF SAVINGS DO YOU"
305  PRINT " HAVE IN MIND? TYPE"
310  PRINT "  1 FOR A SINGLE AMOUNT SAVED"
315  PRINT "  2 FOR A REGULAR AMOUNT MONTHLY"
320  PRINT "  3 FOR A REGULAR AMOUNT WEEKLY"
325  INPUT K
330  IF K=0 THEN 1120
335  IF K=1 THEN 400
340  IF K=2 THEN 400
345  IF K=3 THEN 400
350  PRINT " PLEASE TYPE 1, 2 OR 3
355  GOTO 325
360  REM
400  PRINT " HOW MUCH MONEY DO YOU WANT"
405  PRINT " TO SAVE ";
410  IF K=1 THEN 450
415  IF K=2 THEN 435
420  PRINT " PER WEEK?"
425  LET U$="WEEKS"
430  GOTO 460
435  PRINT " PER MONTH?"
440  LET U$=" MONTHS"
445  GOTO 460
450  PRINT " ?"
455  LET U$="YEARS"
460  PRINT " TYPE THE AMOUNT LIKE THIS:"
465  PRINT " 3.61 FOR 3 POUNDS AND 61 PENCE"
470  REM
475  INPUT P
```

Cont...

```
480  IF P=0 THEN 1120
485  IF P>0 THEN 500
490  PRINT " PLEASE TYPE A POSITIVE AMOUNT"
495  GOTO 475
497  REM
500  PRINT " FOR HOW LONG DO YOU WANT TO SAVE?"
505  PRINT " TYPE THE NUMBER OF ";U$
510  INPUT L
515  IF L=0 THEN 1120
520  IF L>0 THEN 600
525  PRINT " PLEASE TYPE A POSITIVE NUMBER"
530  GOTO 510
535  REM
600  PRINT " WHAT RATE OF INTEREST WILL YOU"
605  PRINT " GET? TYPE THE PER CENT INTEREST PER"
610  PRINT " YEAR (DO NOT TYPE A PERCENTAGE"
615  PRINT " SIGN, JUST THE NUMBER)"
620  INPUT R
625  IF R=0 THEN 1120
630  IF R<0 THEN 645
635  IF R>25 THEN 645
640  GOTO 700
645  PRINT " PLEASE TYPE A SENSIBLE FIGURE"
650  GOTO 620
655  REM
700  PRINT " HOW OFTEN IS INTEREST PAID?"
705  PRINT "   TYPE 1 FOR ONCE A YEAR"
710  PRINT "   TYPE 2 FOR TWICE A YEAR"
715  REM
720  INPUT F
725  IF F=0 THEN 1120
730  IF F=1 THEN 800
735  IF F=2 THEN 800
740  PRINT " PLEASE TYPE 1 OR 2"
745  GOTO 720
750  REM
800  PRINT " WHAT KIND OF REPORT DO YOU WANT?"
805  PRINT "   TYPE 1 FOR A BRIEF REPORT"
810  PRINT "   TYPE 2 FOR A DETAILED REPORT"
815  REM
820  INPUT Y
825  IF Y=0 THEN 1120
830  IF Y=1 THEN 900
835  IF Y=2 THEN 900
840  PRINT " PLEASE TYPE 1 OR 2"
845  GOTO 820
850  REM
900  PRINT " MONEY SAVINGS PLANNER RESULTS"
```

```
905  PRINT
910  IF Y=1 THEN 925
915  PRINT " TIME (";U$;")","AMOUNT SAVED (£)"
920  PRINT
925  IF K=1 THEN 945
930  IF K=2 THEN 980
935  IF K=3 THEN 990
940  REM
945  FOR T=1 TO L STEP 1/F
950  LET A=P*(1+R/(100*F))↑(T*F)
955  IF Y=1 THEN 965
960  PRINT T,INT(100*A+.5)/100
965  NEXT T
970  GOTO 1105
975  REM
980  LET X=12
985  GOTO 995
990  LET X=52
995  LET A=0
1000 FOR T=X/F TO L STEP X/F
1005 LET I=R/(100*F)*(A+P/2*(X/F+1))
1010 LET A=A+P*X/F+I
1015 IF Y=1 THEN 1025
1020 PRINT T,INT(100*A+.5)/100
1025 NEXT T
1030 REM
1035 LET N=L-(T-X/F)
1040 IF N=0 THEN 1105
1045 LET I=R*N/(X*100)*(A+P/2*(N+1))
1050 LET A=A+N*P+I
1055 IF Y=1 THEN 1100
1060 PRINT L,INT(100*A+.5)/100
1065 REM
1100 PRINT
1105 PRINT " AFTER ";L;U$;" YOU WILL HAVE"
1110 PRINT " SAVED £ ";INT(100*A+.5)/100
1115 PRINT
1120 PRINT " DO YOU WANT TO USE THE SAVINGS"
1125 PRINT " PLANNER AGAIN? TYPE YES OR NO"
1130 REM
1135 INPUT R$
1140 IF R$="YES" THEN 300
1145 PRINT
1150 PRINT " END OF PROGRAM REACHED"
1155 PRINT
1160 END
```

Use the savings planner package to help you answer these questions:

1 If you save £20, and get 7% interest, paid once a year, how much will you have after 3 years?

2 Using the amounts from question **1**, how much more will you have if the interest is paid twice a year?

3 If you save £10 and get 12% interest, paid once a year, how much will you have after 5 years?

4 If you save £20 every month for 2 years (2 years = 24 months), and get 8% interest, paid once a year, how much will you have at the end?

5 If you save £1 every week for two years, and get 10% interest, paid twice a year, how much will you have at the end? (Remember 1 year = 52 weeks.)

6 If you get 12% interest paid once a year, how much must you save every month to have £3 000 after 5 years? Solve this by trial and error, starting with £40 per month.

7 At what interest rate will a single sum of money double itself after 8 years? Use £100 as the sum of money and try interest rates around 7%. Try to get two answers: one for interest paid once a year, and one for interest paid twice a year.

8 Find out what interest rates banks, building societies and the Post Office are offering at the moment. Use these interest rates to plan savings of your own.

PACKAGE 5
ARITHMETIC TESTER

This package is designed to improve your ability to do calculations. You are presented with a number of calculations. Each calculation involves two numbers, which may be negative. Work out the calculation and type in your answer. You score a point for a correct answer. If your answer is wrong, the correct answer is displayed.

If you get a division sum, you must work out the answer correct to two decimal places.

You may choose how difficult you want your questions to be. Level 1 uses small numbers, with no negative numbers or fractions. Level 10 uses much bigger numbers, many of which are negative or fractions. You may choose a level between 1 and 10.

1	(lines 200–255)	Display instructions for the use of the program.
2	(lines 300–340)	Initialise the score and the random number generator.
3	(lines 400–475)	Input the required level of difficulty. Use the level to calculate the range of numbers, and the probability of a negative number or fraction.

For each turn:

4	(lines 500–530)	**4.1** Choose two random integers.
		4.2 Change to negative numbers and fractions if necessary.
	(lines 600–680)	**4.3** Choose an operation. Division has half the probability of the other three.
	(lines 700–715)	**4.4** Display the sum and request an answer.
	(line 720)	**4.5** Input the answer.
	(lines 725–780)	**4.6** Check the answer: If it is correct, add 1 to score. If it is wrong, display correct answer.
	(lines 800–810)	**4.7** Display the score
	(lines 815–845)	**4.8** Find out if a change of levels is wanted. If so, go to step **3**.
	(lines 850–870)	**4.9** Find out if another turn is wanted If so, go to step **4**.
5	(lines 875–890)	Display the final score.

Important note

This program uses the RND function to generate random numbers. Unfortunately this function works slightly differently on different computers. Lines 335, 605, 910, 920 and 935 may have to be altered.

Program

```
100 REM INTRODUCING COMPUTERS: PACKAGE 5
105 REM ARITHMETIC TESTER
110 REM WRITTEN BY P.J.BISHOP ON 23/12/79
115 REM
200 REM DISPLAY INITIAL USER INSTRUCTIONS
205 PRINT " THIS PACKAGE IS DESIGNED TO"
210 PRINT " IMPROVE YOUR ABILITY TO DO"
215 PRINT " CALCULATIONS. YOU MAY CHOOSE HOW"
```

Cont...

```
220  PRINT " DIFFICULT YOU WANT YOUR QUESTIONS"
225  PRINT " TO BE. LEVEL 1 USES SMALL NUMBERS,"
230  PRINT " WITH NO NEGATIVE NUMBERS OR"
235  PRINT " FRACTIONS. LEVEL 10 USES MUCH"
240  PRINT " BIGGER NUMBERS, MANY OF WHICH ARE"
245  PRINT " NEGATIVE OR FRACTIONS."
250  PRINT
255  REM
300  REM INITIALISE SCORE AND RANDOM NUMBERS
305  LET K=0
310  LET N=0
315  REM
320  PRINT " TO START THE PROGRAM, TYPE YOUR"
325  PRINT " LUCKY NUMBER FOR TODAY"
330  INPUT Z
335  LET Z=RND(-Z)
340  REM
400  REM INPUT REQUIRED LEVEL OF DIFFICULTY
405  PRINT " HOW DIFFICULT DO YOU WANT YOUR"
410  PRINT " SUMS TO BE? TYPE A NUMBER BETWEEN"
415  PRINT " 1 (EASY) AND 10 (DIFFICULT)"
420  INPUT L
425  IF L<1 THEN 440
430  IF L>10 THEN 440
435  GOTO 455
440  PRINT " PLEASE TYPE A NUMBER BETWEEN"
445  PRINT " 1 AND 10"
450  GOTO 420
455  REM G=PROBABILITY OF NEGATIVE OR FRACTION
460  LET G=(L-1)*.5/9
465  REM E=UPPER LIMIT OF NUMBERS
470  LET E=(L-1)*80/9+20
475  REM
500  REM CHOOSE RANDOM NUMBERS AS REQUIRED
505  GOSUB 900
510  LET A=X
515  GOSUB 900
520  LET B=X
525  IF ABS(B)>ABS(A) THEN 515
530  REM
600  REM CHOOSE OPERATION, CALCULATE ANSWER
605  LET Z=RND(1)
610  IF Z<2/7 THEN 670
615  IF Z<4/7 THEN 655
620  IF Z<6/7 THEN 640
625  LET O$="/"
627  IF B<>0 THEN 630
```

```
628 LET B=.01
630 LET R=INT(A/B*100+.5)/100
635 GOTO 700
640 LET O$="*"
645 LET R=A*B
650 GOTO 700
655 LET O$="-"
660 LET R=A-B
665 GOTO 700
670 LET O$="+"
675 LET R=A+B
680 REM
700 REM DISPLAY SUM, REQUEST ANSWER
705 PRINT
710 PRINT A;" ";O$;" ";B;" = ?"
715 PRINT
720 INPUT S
725 REM CHECK ANSWER
730 IF ABS(S-R)<=ABS(R/10000) THEN 750
735 PRINT
740 PRINT S;" IS WRONG. CORRECT ANSWER IS ";R
745 GOTO 775
750 PRINT
755 PRINT S;" IS CORRECT. WELL DONE"
760 REM UPDATE SCORE
765 LET K=K+1
770 REM
775 LET N=N+1
780 REM
800 REM DISPLAY SCORE
805 PRINT " YOUR SCORE IS ";K;" OUT OF ";N
810 PRINT
815 PRINT " DO YOU WANT TO CHANGE THE LEVEL"
820 PRINT " OF DIFFICULTY OF THE SUMS?"
825 PRINT " TYPE YES OR NO"
830 INPUT R$
835 IF R$="YES" THEN 400
840 REM
845 PRINT
850 PRINT " DO YOU WANT ANOTHER SUM?"
855 PRINT " TYPE YES OR NO"
860 INPUT R$
865 IF R$="YES" THEN 500
870 PRINT
875 PRINT " YOUR FINAL SCORE IS ";K;" OUT OF ";N
880 PRINT
885 STOP
```

Cont...

```
890 REM
900 REM RANDOM NUMBER GENERATOR
905 REM GENERATE RANDOM INTEGER IN RANGE 1 TO E
910 LET X=INT(RND(1)*(E+1))
915 REM CHANGE TO NEGATIVE NUMBER AT RANDOM
920 IF RND(1)>G THEN 930
925 LET X=X*(-1)
930 REM CHANGE TO FRACTION AT RANDOM
935 IF RND(1)>G THEN 945
940 LET X=X/10
945 RETURN
950 REM
955 END
```

PACKAGE 6
CREATE YOUR OWN MODERN ART

This package allows you to assist in the design of a work of modern art, rather like the picture below.

As you can see, the picture consists of a number of bands of contrasting shades. You can decide all the details of the design by answering the questions which are displayed.

After you have answered the questions, the picture you have designed is displayed on the screen. You may then re-design the picture, if you wish.

```
      +  +++++++      +   +  ++++++++      +     +++++
  +          +++ ++++          ++++++  +        +  ++++
          +++++++++        +  +  ++++++++++     +  +++++++
      +     +  +++ ++          +++  ++++    +      +++++++
  +       +++++++++  +          ++++++++   +       ++++++
  +       +++++++       ++    +  ++++++           +++++ +
      +    +++++++       ++   ++++++++  +          +++++++
  +      +++++++              ++++++   +      +++++++
       ++++++++       +    +++++++       +  +++++     +
       +++++++             +++++++        +++++++
    +  +  +++++++       +  +++++++        +++++++
SQUIGGLES
  DO YOU WANT TO DESIGN ANOTHER
  PICTURE? TYPE YES OR NO
```

1	(lines 120–180)	Display initial user instructions.
2	(lines 200–665)	Input and check design details:

N   : number of bands

C$: character used to shade in the bands

S   : straightness of bands

C   : contrast between bands and background

T$. : title for the picture

R   : random number initialiser. Calculate probabilities from these details.

3	(lines 700–1055)	For each line of output:

Adjust width of band using random numbers and probabilities. For each band:

3.1 Output the background area.

3.2 Output the shaded area.

Fill up rest of line with background.

4	(lines 1100–1117)	Output title.
5	(lines 1120–1155)	Find out if user wants to design another picture.

If so, go to step **2**. If not, stop.

Important note

This program makes frequent use of the random number generator RND. Unfortunately this function works slightly differently on different computers. Lines 305, 720, 725, 830, 920 and 1020 may have to be altered.

Program

```
100 REM INTRODUCING COMPUTERS: PACKAGE 6
105 REM CREATE YOUR OWN MODERN ART
110 REM WRITTEN BY P.J.BISHOP ON 20/02/80
115 REM
120 REM DISPLAY INITIAL USER INSTRUCTIONS
125 PRINT " THIS PACKAGE HELPS YOU TO CREATE"
130 PRINT " YOUR OWN MODERN ART. YOU AND THE"
135 PRINT " COMPUTER WILL DESIGN AN ABSTRACT"
140 PRINT " PICTURE, WHICH WILL THEN BE"
145 PRINT " DISPLAYED OR PRINTED . THE PICTURE"
150 PRINT " CONSISTS OF A NUMBER OF BANDS,OF"
155 PRINT " CONTRASTING SHADES. YOU CAN DECIDE"
160 PRINT " ALL THE DETAILS OF THE DESIGN, BY"
```

Cont...

```
165 PRINT " ANSWERING THE QUESTIONS WHICH"
170 PRINT " FOLLOW."
175 PRINT
180 REM
200 REM INPUT AND CHECK DESIGN DETAILS
205 REM SET THE WIDTH OF THE PICTURE
210 REM THIS DETERMINES ALL OTHER DIMENSIONS
215 REM AND DEPENDS ON THE WIDTH OF THE SCREEN
220 REM OF THE COMPUTER IN USE
225 LET W=38
230 PRINT " YOU CAN HAVE BETWEEN 1 AND ";
235 PRINT INT(W/2);" BANDS"
240 PRINT " TYPE THE NUMBER OF BANDS YOU WANT"
245 PRINT
250 INPUT N
255 IF N<1 THEN 270
260 IF N>INT(W/2) THEN 270
265 GOTO 300
270 PRINT
275 PRINT " PLEASE TYPE A NUMBER BETWEEN"
280 PRINT " 1 AND ";INT(W/2)
285 GOTO 245
290 REM
300 PRINT " WHICH CHARACTER DO YOU WANT TO"
305 PRINT " USE TO SHADE IN THE BANDS?"
310 PRINT " TYPE THE CHARACTER YOU WANT"
315 PRINT
320 INPUT C$
325 PRINT " HOW STRAIGHT DO YOU WANT THE"
330 PRINT " BANDS? TYPE A NUMBER BETWEEN 0"
335 PRINT " AND 10, WHERE 0 IS COMPLETELY"
340 PRINT " STRAIGHT, AND 10 IS VERY CURVED"
345 PRINT
350 INPUT S
355 IF S<0 THEN 370
360 IF S>10 THEN 370
365 GOTO 400
370 PRINT " PLEASE TYPE A NUMBER BETWEEN 0"
375 PRINT " AND 10"
380 GOTO 350
385 REM
400 PRINT " HOW MUCH CONTRAST DO YOU WANT"
405 PRINT " BETWEEN THE BANDS AND THE BACK"
410 PRINT "GROUND? TYPE A NUMBER BETWEEN 0"
415 PRINT " AND 10, WHERE 0 IS NO CONTRAST,"
420 PRINT " AND 10 IS COMPLETE CONTRAST"
425 PRINT
430 INPUT C
```

```
435 IF C<0 THEN 450
440 IF C>10 THEN 450
445 GOTO 500
450 PRINT " PLEASE TYPE A NUMBER BETWEEN 0"
455 PRINT " AND 10"
460 GOTO 425
465 REM
500 PRINT " WHAT TITLE DO YOU WANT FOR YOUR"
505 PRINT " PICTURE?"
510 PRINT " PLEASE TYPE YOUR TITLE"
515 PRINT
520 INPUT T$
525 PRINT " TO START THE PICTURE, PLEASE TYPE"
530 PRINT " YOUR LUCKY NUMBER FOR TODAY"
535 PRINT
540 INPUT R
545 PRINT
550 PRINT
555 REM
600 REM INITIALISE RANDOM NUMBER GENERATOR
605 LET X=RND(-R)
610 REM CALCULATE BAND WIDTHS AND PROBABILITIES
615 LET B=INT(W/N)
620 REM B IS INITIAL BAND WIDTH
625 LET P=(10-C)/20
630 REM P IS PROBABILITY OF CHANGING FROM BACK-
635 REM GROUND TO SHADING CHARACTER
640 LET Q=S/10
645 REM Q IS PROBABILITY OF INCREASING OR
650 REM DECREASING BAND WIDTH
655 LET L=INT(W/2)
660 REM L IS NUMBER OF LINES USED FOR PICTURE
665 REM
700 REM START OF OUTPUT FOR EACH LINE
705 FOR K=1 TO L
710 REM ADJUST WIDTH OF BAND
715 REM SELECT RANDOM NUMBER
720 IF RND(1)>Q THEN 750
725 IF RND(1)>0.5 THEN 740
730 LET B=B-1
735 GOTO 750
740 LET B=B+1
745 REM
750 LET A=0
755 REM
800 REM OUTPUT EACH BAND
805 FOR I=1 TO N
810 REM BACKROUND STRIPE
```

Cont . . .

```
815  FOR J=1 TO B/2
820  LET P$=" "
825  REM SELECT RANDOM NUMBER
830  IF RND(1)>P THEN 840
835  LET P$=C$
840  PRINT P$;
845  LET A=A+1
850  IF A>W THEN 1045
855  NEXT J
860  REM
900  REM SHADED STRIPE
905  FOR H=1 TO B/2
910  LET P$=C$
915  REM SELECT RANDOM NUMBER
920  IF RND(1)>P THEN 930
925  LET P$=" "
930  PRINT P$;
935  LET A=A+1
940  IF A>W THEN 1045
945  NEXT H
950  NEXT I
955  REM
1000 REM REST OF LINE
1005 FOR G=A+1 TO W
1010 LET P$=" "
1015 REM SELECT RANDOM NUMBER
1020 IF RND(1)>P THEN 1030
1025 LET P$=C$
1030 PRINT P$;
1035 NEXT G
1040 REM END OF A LINE
1045 PRINT
1050 NEXT K
1055 REM
1100 REM OUTPUT TITLE
1105 PRINT " ";T$
1110 REM PAUSE
1113 FOR Y=1 TO 1000
1115 LET A=A+2-1
1117 NEXT Y
1120 PRINT " DO YOU WANT TO DESIGN ANOTHER"
1125 PRINT " PICTURE? TYPE YES OR NO"
1130 INPUT R$
1135 IF R$="YES" THEN 230
1140 PRINT
1145 PRINT " END OF PROGRAM REACHED"
1150 PRINT
1155 END
```

This chapter has taught you how to use programs which are already loaded onto a computer. This is the way in which many people use computers.

Using packages does not require a detailed knowledge of programming or of computers. Packages enable a large number of people to use computers.

Once you have become familiar with the workings of the package programs, there is no harm in trying a few changes. But please be careful not to introduce errors. Keep a copy of the original program, just in case!

Here are a few suggested changes:

1 The words used by the spelling tester program can be changed. The list of words can be extended up to 100 words. Put the words in the order: wrong spelling, correct spelling, wrong spelling, correct spelling etc. Check the correct spellings in a dictionary.

The list must end with the data: "XXX", "XXX".

2 The words used by the English to French translation program can be changed. The list can be extended up to 100 words. Put the words in the order: English word, French word, English word, French word, etc. Use an English-French dictionary.

The list must end with the data: "XXX," "XXX".

3 The English-French translation program can be changed to translate into another language altogether. Change the word "FRENCH" each time it appears in the program. Change all the French words in the data to the corresponding words in the other language.

4 Extend the wallpaper estimation program to input the price of a roll of the wallpaper and calculate the cost of the number of rolls required. This can be done using the BASIC instructions you learned in chapter **7.**

5 Modify the arithmetic testing program to increase the range of numbers used. In the original form of the program, the range is −100 to +100 at level 10. The range is controlled by line 125 of the program. For example, if you want to extend the range of numbers to −200 to +200. change line 125 to:
```
125 LET   E = (L − 1) * 180/9 + 20
```

6 If you wish to make other changes to the programs, do so extremely carefully.

CHAPTER 10

PUTTING A COMPUTER TO WORK

At the beginning of the book, a computer was described as a data processing machine. In later chapters you learned about the devices which make up a computer, and how some of these devices work. You now know a little about the structure of computers and what they can and cannot do. It is now time to learn how computers are put to work.

The first point to make is that computers never work entirely on their own. Every computer has a number of people working with it, doing several different jobs. Some of these jobs are described in this chapter.

The best way to show how a computer can be put to work, and introduce the people who work with computers, is by an example. The example chosen is typical of many applications of computers in commerce and industry.

COMPUTERISING THE STORES DEPARTMENT

A large engineering works makes a number of metal products. The company has a computer which does its accounts and wages. The computer is a medium sized, fairly reliable machine, which is not fully used all the time.

The company has a problem with its stores department. The stores department keeps a large number of materials, which must be ordered from many different suppliers. All the materials records are kept on paper. Because these records are usually out-of-date, and sometimes incorrect, materials are often out of stock. This causes delays in production, and affects the running of the whole company.

The stores manager realises that something must be done. He wonders if his materials records can be kept on the company's computer. He approaches the person in charge of the computer department – the **data processing manager.**

The data processing manager cannot give an immediate answer, but agrees that the problem is worth investigating. A **systems analyst** is instructed to look into the matter. The systems analyst will decide whether the computer can be used, and if so, how the work can be done. To his dismay, the stores manager learns that this process will take several months.

The systems analyst spends some time in the stores department. He talks to all the people working there, finding out what they do and how they do it. It soon becomes obvious that the computer can be used. The next problem is to find the best way of using it.

The systems analyst spends a few weeks working on a plan for a computerised materials records system. His plan shows what input data is needed, what processing is done and what is the output, and a lot more besides. After several meetings with the stores manager, to work out the details, the plan is accepted.

A team of **programmers** is then given the task of writing the various programs which are needed. As each part of a program is written, it is tested very thoroughly, and corrected, until it is completely free of errors. The programs are put together and tested again.

Time must be booked to run the programs on the computer. These programs are designed to be run once a day. The person in charge of the running of the computer, **the operations manager**, is approached to arrange a suitable time.

Finally, nearly a year after the problem arose, the stores manager has his computerised records system. His department has new forms on which to record the movements of materials. Once a day, the forms are taken to the **data preparation staff** who type the data via visual display terminals onto a magnetic disc. Later in the day, the **computer operators** load the programs, which are kept on another magnetic disc, onto the computer. After the programs have been run, which only takes a few minutes, the operators remove the output from the line printer, and send it to the stores department.

Now the stores manager can see at a glance his up-to-date stock situation. Letters to re-order materials are printed, ready for his signature.

Right *Data preparation staff*

After a few months, the stores manager examines the situation. On two occasions, the computer broke down before his programs were due to run. A **maintenance engineer** was called in to fix the computer. On both occasions the computer was working again after a few hours. The materials records programs were run during the night, and the output was on his desk the next morning.

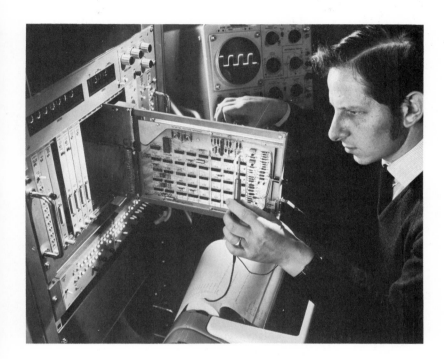

On another occasion something went wrong while his programs were running, and all his data was lost. But copies of the data had been made on magnetic tapes. These tapes were used to restore the data, and his output was only delayed by half an hour.

In spite of these problems, the stores manager decides that the computerised system is much more efficient and more reliable than the previous method of keeping materials records.

EXERCISE

1 a Write down the names of all the jobs mentioned in this chapter.
  b Write a very brief description of what each person does.

2 If it turned out that the computer could not be used to keep the materials records, where would the story have ended?

111

3   Who do you think thought of the idea of keeping copies of the materials records on magnetic tape?

4   Which person would do each of the following jobs?
    a   Supply a line printer with paper.
    b   Correct a computer program.
    c   Decide how to use a computer for a piece of work.
    d   Decide when a program is to be run.
    e   Type input data.

5   Here are some school activities which might be done with the aid of a computer:
    Keeping records of matches played by school teams
    Keeping membership lists of school clubs
    Keeping records of books borrowed from the library

    Choose one of these activities, or make up one of your own. Write a story which tells how you would go about using a computer for the activity.

6   Write a small part of the materials records program mentioned in the text. Input a material code number, quantity in stock, number issued and number received. Calculate the new quantity in stock from this information. Print all the data using suitable headings.

    Suggested letters: C   material code number
                         Q   quantity in stock
                         S   number issued
                         R   number received
                         N   new quantity in stock
    Formula: $N = Q - S + R$

    Modification: Use a loop to make your program process the records for a number of materials.

DATA PROCESSING   The previous section gave an example of how a computer is put to work. The work which computers do is called **data processing**. If a company has a computer, the people who work directly with the computer are in the **data processing department.**

PACKAGES   Not all companies which use computers have a data processing department. Many companies buy all the programs they need with their computer. These programes are called **packages**. Like the packages you used in chapter 9, they are complete, ready-to-use programs. However, they are somewhat longer than the ones in this book!

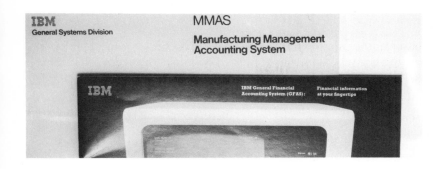

COMPUTER BUREAUS

Other companies send their data processing work to a bureau. A **computer bureau** is a company which does data processing for other companies. A bureau has systems analysts, programmers, computer operators etc. and, of course, a computer.

ANOTHER DATA PROCESSING EXAMPLE

To give you a better idea of how computers are used, another data processing example is now introduced. It describes how computers are used to record bank transactions. Please remember that not all banks use computers in this way, and computers do several other jobs in banking as well as the one described here.

Recording bank transactions
A **transaction** takes place when a person puts money into, or draws money out of their bank account.

The bank's job is to see that each transaction is recorded in the correct account, and that all accounts are kept up to date. This is how it is done:

When money is paid in or taken out, a slip is filled in with the details of the transaction.

DATE _____		BARCLAYS BANK LIMITED **bank giro credit**		Notes: £20	
CREDIT THE ACCOUNT OF _____	DATE _____			Notes: £10	
		CODE NO.	To be used for credit to an account at another branch/Bank	Notes: £5	
Notes: £20				Notes: £1	
Notes: £10		BANK _____		50p	
Notes: £5				Silver	
Notes: £1	CASHIER'S STAMP TO	BRANCH _____ *(block capitals)*		Bronze	
50p				**TOTAL CASH**	
Silver				Postal Orders Cheques, etc. *(Listed overleaf)*	
Bronze	FEE NO. OF ITEMS	ACCOUNT _____		REM £	
TOTAL CASH Postal Orders Cheques, etc., *(Listed overleaf)*		ACCOUNT NO. _____	Paid in by _____		
TOTAL CREDIT £	CT 21				

Later in the same day, information from all the slips at the branch of the bank is typed onto paper tape. This data is then sent by telephone to the bank's computer, where it is copied onto another paper tape.

During the night, the bank's accounts are brought up-to-date. The accounts are kept on magnetic tapes. The transaction data from all the branches is used to produce new copies of the tapes, showing the up-to-date accounts.

A summary of the accounts is printed. This shows the amount of money in each account. Each branch of the bank receives a summary of its accounts early the next day.

At several stages in this process there are checks to ensure that the data is correct. Although these checks cannot detect every possible error, the number of errors which go undetected is extremely small.

SYSTEMS FLOW DIAGRAMS   A convenient way of describing the steps of a data processing task is a **systems flow diagram**. Systems analysts often use systems flow diagrams when planning a data processing task.

Here is a systems flow diagram for recording bank transactions, as described above:

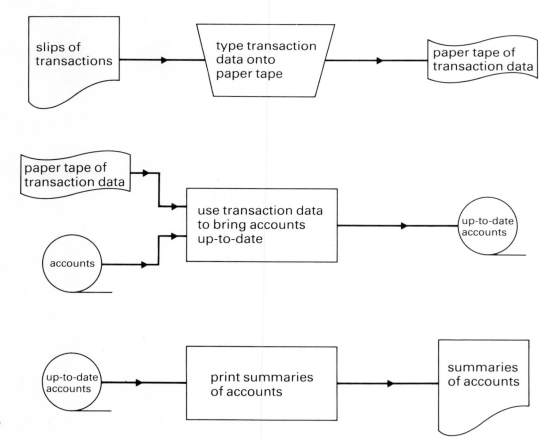

Notice that there is a different symbol for each type of stored data. In practice there are a few other steps concerned with sorting and checking the data. These have been left out of the description and the systems flow diagram for simplicity.

This chapter has shown two ways in which computers are used, and introduced some of the people who work with computers.

It is important to remember that computers can do a very wide variety of work. Many uses of computers are quite similar to the two examples, but many others are very different.

Here are the main points of the chapter again:

- The person who plans how a computer will do a piece of work is called a systems analyst.

- Preparing a task for a computer can take several months.

- Doing something by computer is usually quicker and more reliable (and a lot cheaper) than doing it by hand.

- A systems flow diagram is a convenient way of describing the steps of a data processing task.

1 Answer these questions from the text you have just read:
   a Apart from employing programmers to write its own programs, there are two other ways in which a company can do its data processing. What are the two ways?
   b What is a bank transaction?
   c How is data sent from the branches of some banks to the bank's computer?
   d How are bank accounts stored?
   e What is a systems flow diagram?

2 The shapes of some of the boxes in a systems flow diagram indicate the way in which data is stored. For example, the symbol on the right is for data stored on paper tape.
   a Compare the description of the bank transaction system with its systems flow diagram and work out what each of these boxes represent:

Paper tape symbol

 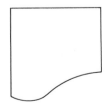

Systems flow diagram symbols

115

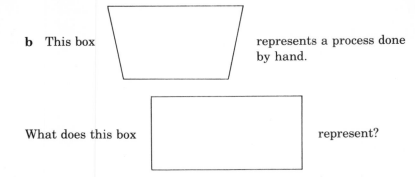

b This box represents a process done by hand.

What does this box represent?

3 The first two steps of many data processing tasks are as follows:

- Type input data from forms onto punched cards.

- Input the data from the punched cards and check it. Print all the data containing errors, and copy the correct data onto a magnetic tape.

The systems flow diagram below shows these steps. Copy it, and write suitable labels in the boxes.

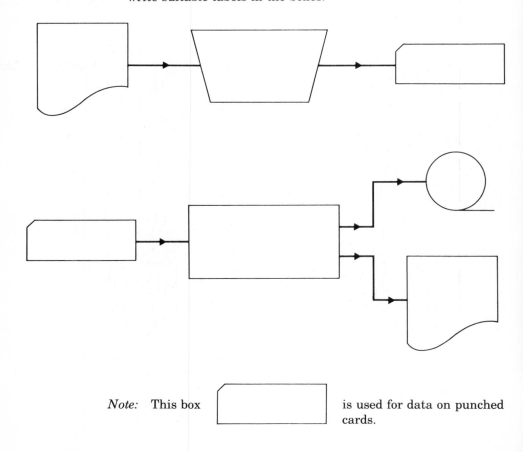

Note: This box is used for data on punched cards.

116

CHAPTER 11

COMPUTERS IN ACTION

This chapter introduces a few of the many ways in which computers are useful tools, helping to get jobs done. You will also find out more about how people work with computers.

Seven examples have been chosen, in an attempt to show the wide variety of jobs done by computers. Please remember that these are not the only ways in which computers are used. There are many areas of industry and commerce where companies without computers are the exception.

AIRLINE RESERVATIONS

Most airlines have booking offices all over the world. At any of these offices it is possible to book seats on any of the airline's flights. For example, someone in Sydney, Australia, might want to book a flight from Sydney to London, and another flight from London to New York. All this can be done from Sydney in a few minutes.

To do this, airlines use a central computer linked to a worldwide communication system. Each booking office is equipped with a number of visual display units linked to the computer. The computer stores details of all forthcoming flights. This data includes flight number, date, time, airports of call, the names of passengers who have already booked seats, and the number of vacant seats. The data is kept on magnetic discs, and can be accessed very quickly.

When a person wants to book a flight, an enquiry is input at the visual display unit. Information about the flight is accessed from the magnetic disc and displayed on the VDU screen.

When a booking is made, the names of the passengers are input at the terminal. They are recorded on the magnetic disc.

In this way, bookings for the same flight can be made from a number of different places all over the world. The amount of paperwork is kept to a minimum.

CONTROLLING MACHINES IN FACTORIES

The machines in most factories have to perform the same operations over and over again. For example, a drilling machine might drill twenty holes, of different sizes, and in different positions, on a part for a motor-car. It then repeats the operations on the next part.

Many machines of this sort are controlled by computers. The most common method is for the computer to produce a paper tape of instructions for the machine. The paper tape is then read by the machine as it works.

A new method is for a machine to have a microprocessor built into it. In this way the machine can be programmed directly. In some factories, there is a minicomputer or microcomputer which is connected directly to a number of machines.

Computer-controlled machines are usually quicker and more accurate than machines controlled by people. However, computer-controlled machines have put a number of people out of work.

All the work to do with driving licences and vehicle licences in Britain is done at a centre in Swansea. Here, a large computer stores all the information about cars, motorcycles and lorries, and the people who drive them. The computer prints drivers' licences and vehicle log books. It records new owners of vehicles, and endorsements on licences.

Keeping all this information on one computer has several advantages. One advantage is the speed with which stolen cars can be traced. However, the computerised system has some disadvantages. For example, it has a reputation for being rather slow.

DRIVER AND VEHICLE LICENCES

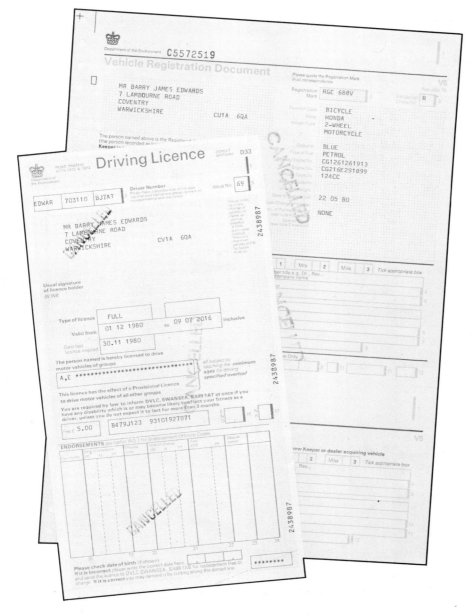

THE BRITISH LIBRARY CATALOGUE

The British Library in London is one of the largest libraries in the world. It has hundreds of thousands of books, in many languages. New books are being added all the time.

All the library's records are kept on a computerised system. The system includes several computers linked together. The computers are accessed by a number of visual display units. The computers do a number of jobs.

Readers can find which books contain the information they want by consulting the library catalogue. This catalogue will eventually contain ten million records. At regular intervals lists of new books are published by the library. These lists are printed by the computer.

THE COMPUTERISED OFFICE

Offices are one of the biggest markets for small computer systems. Computers can speed up the work of an office, and reduce the amount of paperwork.

A typical office computer includes a keyboard for input, a visual display and a printer for output, and several floppy disc drives. (A floppy disc is a small, flexible magnetic disc.) The computer is very simple to use. It is supplied with all the necessary programs.

Office computers are used for storing information, keeping accounts, producing letters, contracts and reports and many other tasks. Although these computers cannot (yet) make the tea, they can keep records of the tea fund!

Letters are no longer typed on paper, but into the computer memory. As it is typed, the letter appears on the visual display screen. Corrections can be made very easily. When the letter is finished, one or more copies can be printed. The letter can also be stored on a disc. Letters can be retrieved from the discs, and altered before being printed. In this way, letters and other documents can be built up from standard paragraphs, with a few changes. Producing letters and documents in this way is called **word processing**.

An office computer makes office work far less repetitive and boring. The work done at the office can be of a much higher standard than before. On the other hand, this type of computer is reducing the number of office jobs available.

How can you gamble without ever losing your money? The answer is to buy Premium Bonds.

ERNIE

Buying Premium Bonds is rather like putting money in a bank. Your money is safe, and you can draw it out at any time. However, you do not get any interest. Instead, there is a lottery every week. Every month there is a top prize of £250 000. There are many other prizes. The more Premium Bonds you have, the greater your chance of winning.

How are the winners selected? This is where ERNIE the computer comes in. The winners are selected by choosing **random numbers**, rather like drawing numbers out of a hat. ERNIE has a special piece of hardware called an Electronic Random Number Indicator to pick the random numbers. The hardware is designed to be completely fair. No one can predict which numbers will be selected, or influence the selection in any way.

ERNIE does much more than just select the winners. ERNIE keeps all the records of how many Premium Bonds everyone has. ERNIE also deals with changes of address, and the buying and selling of Bonds.

Because of the way ERNIE works, if you win one week, you have the same chance of winning again the next week!

One day, the person with whom you go out for an evening might be chosen by a computer. Sounds ridiculous? Not any more. Matching people by computer is a large and expanding business. This is how the system works:

Men or women who want to use the computer dating system first fill in a form. The form contains a number of questions about themselves, their interests, their likes and dislikes. The information is input into a computer. It is used as data by a number of programs which match people who are suited to each other. Each person is then sent a list of the names and telephone numbers of some suitable partners. It is then up to the people to get in touch with each other.

END-OF-CHAPTER SUMMARY   The examples introduced in this chapter have given you a glimpse of some of the many ways in which computers are being put to work. From the examples you can see how wide the range of computer applications is.

Some applications have replaced manual systems with computerised systems. Other applications depend entirely on computers. They have only come about since the invention of computers.

These examples also show some of the ways in which people work with computers. Not all the people who work with computers are programmers or systems analysts. Many of the people who work with computers do not know very much about how computers work.

One final point to remember is that computers are general-purpose machines. The same computer can perform a very wide variety of tasks. Several of the applications described in this chapter could use the same kind of computer.

EXERCISE   1   Answer these questions from the text of this chapter.
    a   Which device is used for the input of data by an airline reservation system?
    b   How is airline reservation data stored?
    c   How do many computer-controlled machines 'read' their instructions?
    d   What is the latest development in computer-controlled machines?
    e   What is one advantage of keeping records of all vehicle and driver licences in one place?
    f   Name two jobs done by the British Library computer system.
    g   Name two advantages of office computers.
    h   What hardware does a typical office computer contain?
    i   How are letters typed on an office computer?
    j   What is ERNIE?

2   Think of working as secretary or typist in an office with a computer. Compare it to working in an office without a computer.
    a   Which job do you think would be more interesting?
    b   Which job do you think would be more difficult?
    c   Which job do you think would need more training?
    d   Which job would you prefer? Give your reasons.

3   Here are a few more ways in which computers are used. Find out more about these applications of computers.
Medicine, police work, space exploration, weather forecasting, military applications.

4   Find out what people with motorbike or car licences think about these being produced by a computer. Discuss your findings.

5   Give your views on the idea of computer dating.

CHAPTER 12
A BRIEF HISTORY OF COMPUTERS

As with many things, it is difficult to say when computers began. Electronic computers have been with us for just over thirty years. However, the ideas behind computers go back several centuries.

Many people have helped computers develop. Some of these people are mentioned in this chapter. The growth of computers has also depended on inventions, like that of transistors. Every now and then a computer is built which represents a step forward in computer design. Some of these computers are mentioned in this chapter.

THE FIRST STEPS TOWARDS COMPUTERS

People have always found calculations difficult. Over the centuries many devices have been invented to help with calculations. These devices are the earliest ancestors of computers.

The oldest known calculating device is the **abacus**. It uses beads threaded on wires to represent numbers. Calculations are done by moving the beads. The abacus has been in use for thousands of years.

During the seventeenth century three important calculating devices were invented. The first was by John Napier, the inventor of logarithms. In 1617, Napier designed a set of rods, called **Napier's bones**, to make multiplication easier. The rods can be arranged to form a multiplication table.

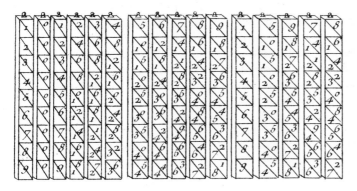

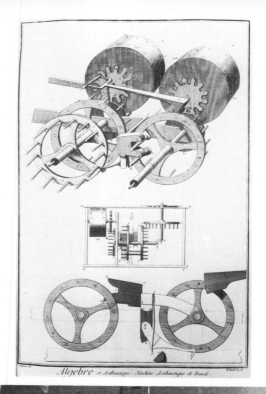

Top *An engraving showing the workings of Pascal's adding machine*
Centre *A Leibnitz adding machine*

The second invention was by Blaise Pascal, a Frenchman. He designed and built an adding machine, using toothed wheels, in 1642. The machine could add and subtract, but it could not multiply or divide.

The third invention was by Gottfried von Leibnitz, in Germany, in 1671. His machine could add, subtract, multiply and divide. It also used toothed wheels.

Over the years these machines were copied and improved. At first they were made by hand. Later they were made in factories, using machine tools. These machines have survived up to the present, in the form of the cash registers. However, mechanical cash registers are rapidly being replaced by electronic ones.

As you should know by now, computers can do much more than just calculate. Information processing by machine had its origins in the nineteenth century. The first developments took place in a rather unlikely area of work – weaving.

A woven pattern on cloth can be produced by raising or lowering threads of different colours as each row of the cloth is woven. With hundreds of threads involved, this process can get extremely complicated. The first device to carry out this process automatically was invented by a French textile manufacturer, Joseph Jacquard, in about 1802.

Jacquard used punched cards to store the information needed to weave patterns. The cards were read automatically by weaving machines to control the raising and lowering of threads.

Although Jacquard's system was very efficient, it needed fewer people to work with the looms. There were riots when the looms were first introduced. In the town of Lyon, some of the looms were burned. However, these machines soon became very popular. Many looms based on Jacquard's design are still in use today.

THE EARLY DAYS OF INFORMATION PROCESSING

JOSEPH JACQUARD

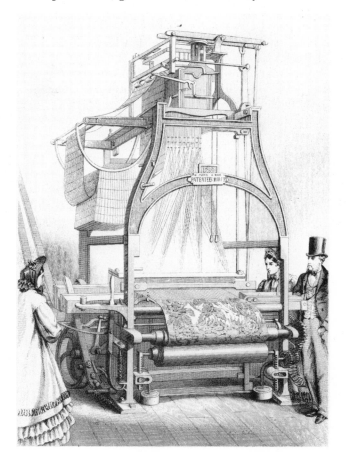

Left   *A Jacquard loom*

CHARLES BABBAGE

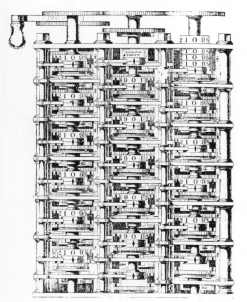

Charles Babbage has been called 'the father of computers'. He designed a machine called the **Analytical Engine** in 1834. This device used toothed wheels for calculations, and punched cards for data storage. It was the first machine to have input, processing and output devices. It was also the first calculating machine which could be programmed.

Left   *Analytical Engine*
Right   *Charles Babbage*

However, the Analytical Engine was impossible to build. The parts it required could not be made accurately enough by the craftsmen of the time. Almost one hundred years were to pass before Babbage's ideas could be put into practice.

HERMAN HOLLERITH

The next big step forward in the development of information processing took place in the USA. In the USA, a population census is held every ten years. Towards the end of the nineteenth century, the population was growing rapidly. Processing of the census information was taking longer and longer. It was feared that processing of information from the 1890 census would take more than ten years.

Herman Hollerith devised a method of storing the census information on punched cards. He invented machines, called **tabulators,** to process data from the cards. Hollerith's invention enabled the 1890 census results to be ready after only three years.

Hollerith punched card sorting machine

128

Hollerith formed a company to market punched cards and tabulating machines. His company later became part of IBM, the largest computer company in the world.

1 Arrange these devices in order of age, from the oldest to the most recent:
Napier's bones, tabulator, abacus, cash register, Analytical Engine, Pascal adding machine, Jacquard loom, Leibnitz calculator.

2 Who:
   a invented logarithms?
   b designed a machine which could not be constructed at the time?
   c helped weaving and information processing with one invention?
   d speeded up the work of the USA census in 1890?
   e first thought of the ideas of input, processing and output?

3 After the Leibnitz calculator, which other devices mentioned in the text could calculate?

4 If you had a business, what machines would have been available to help with your accounts in each of the following years?
   a 1510
   b 1710
   c 1910

5 Which was the first programmable computer to be designed?

THE ELECTRONIC AGE BEGINS

All the devices mentioned up to now were mechanical. They used toothed wheels and other moving parts to store and process information. In the early years of the twentieth century, valves and magnetic recording devices were invented. Electronic computers, with no moving parts, now became a possibility.

An early magnetic recording machine, once used by the BBC, which used steel ribbon instead of tape.

THE THEORY OF COMPUTERS

Computers do not work by magic. The way computers work is based on a theory of computing. This theory has been built up over the years by a number of people, starting with Charles Babbage. Three other people have made very important contributions – George Boole, Alan Turing and John von Neumann.

Left   *George Boole*
Centre *Alan Turing*
Right   *John von Neuman*

In 1847, George Boole worked out the system of logic which forms the basis of the design of all computers.

In 1937, Alan Turing worked out what a computing machine could and could not do.

In 1946, John von Neumann set out the general principles of the design of a computer. All modern computers are based on the work of these men.

The Second World War created an urgent demand for computers. Computers were needed for codebreaking, and for calculations to do with navigation, firing guns, dropping bombs, and moving supplies. By the end of the war, computers had been developed in Germany, the USA and Britain. These were the first electronic computers.

These computers were very crude objects by today's standards. They were very large, contained miles of wire, and used valves. We now know them as **first generation** computers.

Some of the more famous first generation computers are mentioned below. You will see that they have very strange names.

The **Z3** and **Z4** computers were designed by Konrad Zuse in Germany during the war. Unfortunately they were destroyed by Allied bombing. Little is known about them.

In Britain, the **Colossus** computer was used for codebreaking from 1943 to the end of the war. In the USA there was the **ASCC** in 1944, which still had moving parts, and the **ENIAC** in 1946, which was a fully electronic computer.

Below *The ENIAC computer*

Shortly after the war ended, four more computers were completed. These were **Manchester University Mark 1** (1948), **EDSAC** (1949), **EDVAC** (1950) and **ACE** (1951).

The computers constructed up to this time were all scientific machines. They were used to carry out long and difficult calculations. They were all based at universities or military establishments.

COMPUTERS MOVE INTO
COMMERCE

A few people soon realised how useful computers would be in business. The **LEO** computer in Britain, and the **UNIVAC** computer in the USA, both went into service in 1951. They were the first commercial computers. Soon they had proved their worth.

Other companies started producing business computers. These included **IBM**, **Honeywell**, and **Burroughs** in the USA, and **GEC**, **Elliot** and **ICT** (later **ICL**) in Britain.

The market for business computers has grown ever since.

THE INVENTION OF TRANSISTORS

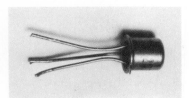

Above   *A valve and a transistor*
Right   *Atlas, a second generation computer*

All the first generation computers used valves for information processing. Valves are large, and use a lot of electricity. They give off a considerable amount of heat, and do not last very long.

In 1948 the **transistor** was invented at the Bell Telephone Laboratories in the USA.

In a computer, a transistor does the same job as a valve. But transistors use far less electricity, and are much smaller and more reliable than valves. Transistors are also much cheaper than valves.

Computers using transistors soon became available. We now know them as **second generation** computers. Second generation computers soon replaced first generation computers, which used valves.

SECOND GENERATION COMPUTERS

Second generation computers were smaller, faster, more reliable and cheaper than first generation computers. Improvements were made in software, making these computers easier to use. High level languages were introduced, to speed up programming. This was an improvement over the low-level languages used by first generation computers.

During this period (the late 1950's and early 1960's), computers spread very rapidly. Many companies changed to computers, with varying degrees of success. In some companies, the change to computers had been carefully planned. People in the company had learned about computers, and knew what they could and could not do. In most of these companies, computers brought greater efficiency and helped the business to grow.

In other companies, the change to computers was not carefully planned. Often the wrong type of computer was bought. The change to computers brought difficulties, delays and loss of business. This is happening less often now, as people are getting more used to computers.

As computers were becoming more popular, they were being improved all the time. The next big improvement was the **integrated circuit**, or **chip**. An integrated circuit is a single component containing a number of transistors. Integrated circuits are smaller, cheaper and more reliable than single transistors. The first computers to use integrated circuits were sold in 1964.

Once again prices of computers came down, and sales increased. Minicomputers became very popular, being cheap enough for small firms to afford.

An integrated circuit (chip)

We have now reached the stage of an entire central processing unit on a single chip. Such a chip is called a **microprocessor**. It contains thousands of transistors and other components.

THE MICROPROCESSOR REVOLUTION

Microprocessors first became available in 1972. They are used in calculators, cameras, control equipment and electronic games as well as in computers. In the near future, they will be used in cars, cookers, central heating control systems and in many other ways. It is expected that microprocessors will have a big impact on the way we live.

Computers which use microprocessors are called **microcomputers**. Microcomputers are cheap, easy to use and reliable. They are widely used in schools, colleges and universities, as well as in offices and factories. Some people have microcomputers in their homes.

Microprocessors have brought about yet another decrease in the cost of computers. It remains to be seen just how low the price of computers will go.

This brings the story of computers up to the present, but it does not end here. Many people are working to develop new ideas in computing. New uses are being found for computers. More and more computers are being produced, sold and put to work. Computers are becoming an essential part of our everyday lives.

END-OF-CHAPTER SUMMARY

This chapter has traced the history of computers, from thousands of years ago to the present. Broadly speaking, there have been three phases. These are:

- The early work on mechanical calculators by people such as Napier, Pascal, and Leibnitz.

- The foundations of information processing, by Jacquard, Hollerith and Babbage during the nineteenth century.

- The very rapid development of electronic computers since the Second World War.

Electronic computers have developed in four stages:

- First generation computers, using valves

- Second generation computers, using transistors

- Third generation computers, using integrated circuits

- The microprocessor revolution, with complete central processing units on one chip.

EXERCISE

1 Name four people who made important contributions to the theory of computers.

2 Why was so much work done on computers during the Second World War?

3 Write down the names of some first generation computers.

4 Which invention marked the start of the second generation of computers?

5   Name two early commercial computers.

6   Name some companies which produce commercial computers.

7   Which invention marked the start of the third generation of computers?

8   Give some reasons for the decrease in cost of computers.

9   Write a war story, taking place in 1945, which includes a computer in the plot.

10   Compare the photographs of first generation computers with the ones of modern computers elsewhere in the book. What differences do you notice?

Bottom   *The Ace Computer (1951)*
Top   *The Colossus code-breaking computer (1943)*

CHAPTER 13

COMPUTERS IN SOCIETY

This chapter looks at the part played by computers in a modern society such as Britain. The Computer Revolution of today is compared with the Industrial Revolution of two hundred years ago. Your attention is drawn to some social problems resulting from the widespread use of computers. These problems include loss of privacy, unemployment and increased political control by governments and police forces. Finally there is a look ahead, over the next fifty years or so. This gives some idea of the way in which computers, and societies, might develop.

Some very difficult problems are mentioned in this chapter. Many of them have no obvious answers. The aim of this chapter is to tell you a little about the problems, and then leave you to make up your own mind about ways to solve them.

TODAY'S WORLD OF CHANGE

Modern society is very complicated. The photographs on the right show just a few aspects of it. Although modern society is there for all of us to see, it is very difficult to understand.

Many factors influence modern society. Computers are just one of these factors. Some of the other influences can be seen in the photographs.

When thinking of the influence of computers on society, it is important to remember that computers are not the only influence. This is why some parts of this chapter are not directly about computers.

One fact about modern society is quite clear. It is a world of change. This change is usually caused by advances in medicine or technology. On the one hand, change brings new opportunities and a higher standard of living for some people. On the other hand, change leaves other people behind. Change makes some people feel insecure and anxious. They are sometimes unable to cope. Computers must take part of the blame for this.

To explore the theme of change a little further, the next section looks at another time of rapid social change – the Industrial Revolution. The Industrial Revolution is then compared with the Computer Revolution.

THE INDUSTRIAL REVOLUTION

The Industrial Revolution started about two hundred years ago. It was brought about by the use of steam power, and the invention of large numbers of machines. These machines replaced muscle power and hand tools. They also began to do a number of tasks that would have been impossible using manual labour. The Industrial Revolution is still going on today. Machines are being improved, and new machines are being developed all the time.

The Industrial Revolution brought about a number of very far-reaching social changes. Work moved from homes to factories, loosening family ties. Many people were freed from strenuous manual labour. However, working with machines was often in crowded, dirty and dangerous conditions. Small, closely-knit communities were replaced by large, impersonal masses of people. Huge slums developed as people crowded into cities. In many areas, pollution was far worse than it is today. A few people did very well, while many people struggled to survive.

As time went by, living conditions and standards of education and health improved. Trade unions were formed to protect the interests of working people. The Industrial Revolution has led to an abundance of cheap manufactured goods.

The increasing use of computers during the last thirty years has been called **'The Computer Revolution'**, or 'The Second Industrial Revolution'. The Computer Revolution is rather like the Industrial Revolution. Machines replaced human muscles doing boring, repetitive physical tasks. Computers have replaced human brains doing boring, repetitive mental tasks. Like machines, computers have made possible some tasks which could not have been done without them. However, this comparison must not be taken too far. Remember that computers are also machines, and cannot think for themselves.

Like the Industrial Revolution, the Computer Revolution is still going on. The most recent stage of development of computers – the introduction of microprocessors – has been called **'The Microprocessor Revolution'**. Many people think that microcomputers and other devices using microprocessors will have a bigger social impact than earlier types of computers.

What about the social effects of the Computer Revolution? Machines took people away from physical labour and put them into factories. Some people claim that computers are taking people away from many kinds of jobs and putting them in dole queues. In a short space of time during the Industrial Revolution, machines changed almost every aspect of society. Will computers have the power to bring about similar changes? If so, what are these changes? This chapter looks at these questions, but many of them have no simple answers.

EXERCISE

1 Answer these questions from the text you have just read.
   a About how long ago did the Industrial Revolution start?
   b About how long ago did the Computer Revolution start?
   c What was the main cause of the Industrial Revolution?
   d What were some of the benefits of the Industrial Revolution?
   e What were some of the disadvantages of the Industrial Revolution?
   f Are the problems raised by the use of computers easy to solve?

2 Find out more about some of these topics:
   a The advantages and disadvantages of the Industrial Revolution.
   b Similarities between the Computer Revolution and the Industrial Revolution.
   c The Microprocessor Revolution.

3 A number of inventions in the twentieth century have had a big influence on the way we live. These inventions include the motor car, the aeroplane and the television.
   a Discuss (or write about) the influence of these inventions. Try to imagine how things would be without them.

b Make a list of other inventions which have had a big influence on the way we live.

c Make a list of things which you think might be invented in the future.

4 Find out from an old person, or several old people:
a What they know about computers.
b What they think about computers.
c Whether they like things to change.

5 At one stage during the Industrial Revolution a group of people called the Luddites was set up to oppose the spread of machines. Some members of the group went around smashing machines.

Do you think that computers will ever be treated this way? Discuss or write about your opinion.

6 'The microprocessor will do to people what the motor car did to horses'. Discuss.

SOME PROBLEMS CAUSED BY COMPUTERS

People have worried about computers ever since computers were first invented. These anxieties are made worse by the fact that many people know very little about computers. Perhaps it is quite right that people should be worried. Computers are helping to cause several serious social problems. The worst of these problems are unemployment, loss of privacy and increased political control by governments and police forces. These problems are now discussed.

The Story of Bill Jones

Bill Jones was very good with his hands. In his spare time, he used to build model boats. He would spend months on each model, working away until it was perfect in every detail.

Bill used to work in a factory. He was in charge of a milling machine. Under his skilled hands, his machine would cut and shape pieces of metal.

He worked patiently at each piece until he was satisfied. Every few months, an apprentice would be assigned to help him, and study the way he worked. In this way his skill was passed on to others.

Then things changed. Bill's milling machine was scrapped. It was replaced by a new automatic machine. All Bill had to do was put the blocks of metal on the machine and push a button. A paper tape controlled the working of the machine. The new machine worked much faster, but when Bill took the finished piece off the machine, you could see he was not satisfied. But Bill was not a person to complain. He kept his skill for his models.

Then things changed again. A computer was installed in the machine shop. It controlled all the milling machines. The machines were automatically supplied with blocks of metal. The finished pieces were removed automatically. Bill lost his job.

The redundancy pay helped, but Bill was too close to retiring age to get another job. Besides, nobody wanted skilled machine operators any more. Computers were used instead.

Do you know someone like Bill Jones? It is quite likely that you do, because the same thing has happened to thousands of people. In offices and factories in Britain and many other countries, people have been put out of work by computers.

But this is not the whole story. Computers put people out of work, but they also create jobs. You learned about some of these jobs in a previous chapter. These jobs are highly skilled and well paid, but fewer in number than the jobs which are lost.

Also, many firms depend on their computers. Without their computers, the firms would have to close down. Large numbers of jobs would then be lost. Computers have helped many firms to grow and prosper. In this way, jobs have been created.

Because of their efficiency and productivity, computers help the economies of many countries. Countries like Britain, the USA and Japan export computers. This brings money into these countries, and also helps their economies.

Trade unions are divided in their attitudes to computers. Some trade unions oppose computers because of the unemployment they cause. Other unions see the advantages of computers, especially their greater efficiency. They realise that computers help firms to grow, and in this way create jobs.

Thus you can see that there is no simple answer to the problem of computers and unemployment. What do you think?

LOSS OF PRIVACY

All about Eileen Atkins

Eileen Atkins was furious. She had applied for a loan to buy an automatic washing machine, and her request had been refused. She telephoned the finance company to find out the reasons for their refusal. This is what she was told:

We checked up on your bank, and they told us that you have been overdrawn twice in the last six months. Your insurance company informed us that you were late paying your premium this month. Your doctor mentioned that you have been ill several times recently. We also found out that you have an endorsement on your driving licence and were in trouble with the police when you were young.

With all this against you, we do not feel able to give you the loan. And you can't argue against these facts. All that information is stored on computers.

Luckily, stories like this cannot happen – yet. But one part of the story is true. All the information mentioned is already being stored on computers. However, at the present time, the information is not available to anyone who asks for it.

Many people are worried about the enormous amount of personal information that is being stored on computers. How safe is this information? Who can see it? Can it be passed from one computer to another? These are difficult questions to answer.

The computer systems which process personal information have safeguards built into them. These are to stop the information falling into the wrong hands. Banks, hospitals and insurance companies are very careful about the personal information they have. Nevertheless, it is possible, in theory, to get this information from the computers very quickly. And in Britain there is no law to protect personal information at present.

Like unemployment, the possible loss of privacy caused by computers is a very difficult question. What do you think?

January 13th, 1984

It was 3 a.m. and bitterly cold. At a given signal, figures in dark overcoats moved out of the shadows. The door burst open on the impact of a strong shoulder. The people inside the house were dragged from their beds and bundled into a car. Minutes later they were at the headquarters. As the light shone in their eyes they were told:

'We know all about you. We know where you have been. We know the people you have met. We have copies of all the letters you have sent and received. We have printouts of all your telephone conversations. We know all your plans. We have arrested all your friends. All the information about you is stored on our computers. Now confess.'

George Orwell wrote a very famous book called *1984*. In his book is a leader called Big Brother. Big Brother controls everyone completely, even what they think. Will computers enable governments to get like this? Some people think so.

In Britain, the government has a number of computers. The police have several, including one used by the Special Branch. No doubt these contain as much information as possible about spies, hijackers, and terrorists. But what about ordinary people?

In Britain, everyone has a right to say whatever they think is true. It doesn't matter whether they support the government, or oppose it. There are organisations like the National Council for Civil Liberties which make sure that this right is preserved. At present there is no evidence of people getting into trouble because of information about them stored on government or police computers. But will things stay as they are?

Unfortunately, the picture is very different in other countries. In some countries, secret police use computers to help keep track of opponents of the government. These people are often arrested and imprisoned without trial, and sometimes tortured and killed.

1 Answer these questions from the text you have just read.   **EXERCISE**
  a Do computers put some people out of work?
  b How do computers help to create jobs?
  c Do all trade unions oppose computers?
  d Who owns the computers which store personal information?
  e Is there a law in Britain to protect personal information stored on computers?

f Which organisation looks after people's rights of free speech in Britain?

g Who is Big Brother?

2 Here are some topics to write about or discuss:
   a Your own views about computers and unemployment.
   b Your own views about computers and loss of privacy.
   c Whether the police should be allowed to gather and store any information they like.
   d Will Britain have a Big Brother in 1984?
   e Whether the police and the Special Branch should have computers.
   f Many of the computers used by governments and secret police in other countries are made in Britain. Is it right to export computers for this sort of purpose?

3 The names of a few trade unions are:
   TGWU: Transport and General Worker's Union.
   NALGO: National Association of Local Government Officers.
   APEX: Association of Professional and Executive Staff. This union includes many computer workers.
   NGA: National Graphical Association.
   Try to find out the attitudes of these (or other) unions towards computers.

4 Russia and Chile are two countries where secret police use computers to store information on opponents of the government. Try to find out which other countries do this.

An organisation which helps political prisoners all over the world is called Amnesty International. This organisation can possibly supply more information about the use of computers for political purposes.

5 In 1979, there was a strike by a small number of Post Office computer operators. It prevented the Post Office from sending out hundreds of millions of pounds worth of telephone bills. Find out more about what happened, and write about, or discuss the matter.

6 Unemployment, loss of privacy and increased political control by governments are three social problems made worse by computers. Can you think of any others?

7 The USA and Sweden are two countries which have laws about the storage of personal information. Find out which other countries have similar laws, and more about the laws.

8 It has been suggested that people should have the right to see their own medical records, social security records and employer's records about them. Discuss this suggestion.

9 Make up a story of your own involving people and computers in some situation. Your story can be set in the present or at some time in the future.

10 Would you like everyone to know:
   a How much money you have in the bank?
   b What illnesses you have had?
   c How old you are?
   d Whether you have been in trouble with the police?

   Compare your own answers to these questions with other people's answers.

11 The British Computer Society is an association of people who work with computers. One of its projects is to help disabled people get jobs working with computers. Find out more about this project.

A Happy New Year

'A happy new year, George, and to you, Mary'.

George and Mary Thomas smiled at each other as their HELPMATE home computer turned up the lights in their room. It was January 1st, 2001. In a few minutes their breakfast was ready.

Mary told HELPMATE to run her bath, while George asked to be reminded of his appointments for the day. Some mail had arrived, and HELPMATE asked whether he should print it or read it to them.

They were expecting guests for lunch. Mary could not remember what kind of food their guests preferred. HELPMATE contacted the computer at their friends house to find out, and then ordered the necessary ingredients. When the food had arrived, Mary entered a new menu into the cooking program. She wanted to surprise her friends.

After lunch, George did some work. He linked his home terminal to his work computer, and called up three of his colleagues on the videophone for a conference. Afterwards he used the word processing facility to assemble a contract, which he dispatched to his colleagues for their comments.

George and Mary decided to go out for their evening meal. HELPMATE booked a table at a restaurant, and sent for an autotaxi. Programmed with the address of the restaurant, the electric autotaxi carried them quickly and quietly to their destination.

They were most amused to find that the restaurant still used old fashioned methods. There were waiters, and even a chef. They agreed that it made an interesting change.

When they got home, HELPMATE asked them whether they had enjoyed themselves....

What a way to see the new year in ...

Brian Roberts looked up from his work as he realised it was past midnight. It was now January 1st, 2001. It would be six hours before his shift finished.

As he fitted rows of type into the block that would print a page of the day's newspaper, Brian felt proud. Twenty-two years ago, in 1979, his union had been the first to oppose the spread of computers, because they took away people's jobs. After a strike of eleven months, they had succeeded. In the years which followed, other unions had done the same. Now, computers were rare. They had been forced back to the places where they came from – universities and research establishments.

But the struggle had been long and bitter. Companies had been forced to get rid of computers and other automatic equipment, and hire more workers. In the process, wages had stopped rising, and a recession had set in.

Although most people now had jobs, life was hard. Most jobs were dull and boring. Many high-quality goods which had been available could no longer be made. Credit cards had disappeared, and cheques took weeks to clear. Holidays abroad were out of the question.

As Brian carried on working, he remembered that his last wage packet had been wrong. Somebody in the wages department couldn't add up. Now if it was done by computer ...

These two stories show how difficult it is to predict the future. Some people would believe the first story, other people would believe the second story. Most people would not believe either story. They would say that the truth lies somewhere between the two.

Leaving aside this uncertainty for a moment, there are several predictions which can be made about computers.

In the next twenty years, computers will continue to get faster, smaller, cheaper and more efficient. Voice recognition and computer graphics are big growth areas. New kinds of storage such as magnetic bubble memories and integrated circuits which work at very low temperatures will probably come into use.

It will become easier to use a computer. Computers will be used in more and more applications, and affect more and more people. Microprocessors will be built into a wide variety of devices. Computing could become the world's largest single industry.

This leads back to the original questions – what is the limit to the spread of computers? At the moment, no one knows. In the next twenty years, it will be up to all of us to choose how far we want computers to spread. The more people who know something about computers, the easier these choices will be.

Computers are not the only influence in a changing world. To get a better idea of the development of computers, one must ask – in what kind of a world will this development take place?

In Britain and other industrial countries, the standard of living will probably continue to increase. Pay will improve, working hours will get shorter and holidays will get longer. People may have to stay at school longer. No doubt there will be new inventions, and new advances in knowledge.

But inflation, pollution, unemployment and crime will continue to be problems. Petrol and natural gas will become very scarce. The threat of nuclear war will still be there.

In the rest of the world, some advances will no doubt be made in living standards, but problems will continue. Food shortage, disease and overpopulation will continue to be major problems. In the next forty years, the world's population will probably double. Most of the increase will be in poor countries. (Britain's population is hardly increasing at all.)

What effect will computers have on the world of the future? No one knows for sure, but here is a useful guideline: Computers must be used to serve people, and not the other way round.

Left *Magnetic bubble memory device*
Right *A Josephson junction integrated circuit which works at very low temperatures*

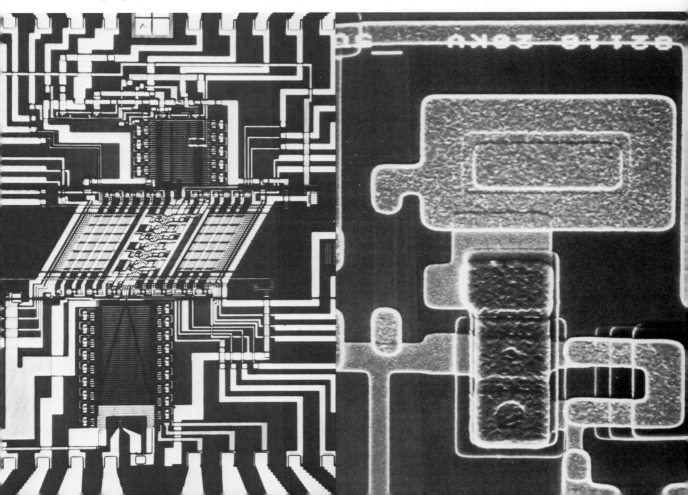

1 These questions are based on the story of George and Mary Thomas.

    a Make a list of all the things which their HELPMATE home computer did.

    b What other things do you think their computer could do?

    c How many of the things that HELPMATE did can be done by present-day computers?

    d Do you think that everyone in the society would be able to live like George and Mary Thomas?

    e Would you like to live in that kind of society? Give reasons for your answer.

2 These questions are based on the story of Brian Roberts.

    a What is a recession? The last major recession in Britain was in the 1930's. Find out what happened then.

    b In what ways is life in this story different from life today?

    c Where were computers still used?

    d Would you like to live in that kind of society? Give reasons for your answers.

3 How do you think life will be in Britain in the year 2001? Write your own story of how some people spend January 1st, 2001.

or

Work out how old you will be on January 1st, 2001. Write a story about yourself on that day.

4 Use the text of this section and your own ideas to answer these questions:

    a List some ways in which the standard of living in Britain will probably improve in the next twenty years.

    b List some problems which Britain will still face in twenty years time.

5 Discuss, or write about, some of these topics:

    a Future applications of computers.

    b The impact of microcomputers in the future.

    c Ways in which the information in this chapter has changed your attitude to computers.

6 The chances are that you will have to do two or three kinds of jobs during your working life. Write down, or discuss your feelings about this.

CHAPTER 14

CONCLUSION: A SECOND LOOK AT COMPUTERS

This chapter takes a second look at some of the main points made in the book. Ideas from different parts of the book are drawn together. It is hoped that this will leave you feeling confident about what you know about computers.

In this chapter, four questions are considered. Some of them are the same as the ones in the first chapter. The questions are:

- What is a computer?

- How does a computer work?

- What can and can't a computer do?

- What effects are computers having?

WHAT IS A COMPUTER?

A computer is an electronic machine which automatically inputs and processes information and outputs the results of the processing. A computer is controlled by a program which is stored inside it.

Automatic means that a computer can carry out all the steps of a task on its own. But a computer cannot work entirely on its own. People write the programs, prepare the data, operate the computer and interpret the results.

Electronic means that inside a computer there are no moving parts. All processing of data is done by electricity moving through solid state components.

Information processing covers a very wide range of activities, from producing wage slips to controlling spacecraft. Most computers are general purpose machines, capable of a variety of tasks.

Machine means that in some ways a computer is like a drill, washing machine or sewing machine. Like all machines, a computer is a device which helps to get things done.

HOW DOES A COMPUTER WORK?

A useful computer consists of hardware and software. Each has a part to play in the working of a computer.

The **hardware** of a computer is its integrated circuits, input, output and storage devices. Using pulses of electricity or small magnetised spots to represent data, the hardware carries out each step of an information processing task.

The **software** of a computer is the instructions which tell the hardware what to do. There are several different kinds of software. Some software is for specific tasks, like calculating wages. Other software controls the way a computer works, making it easier to use. All the software which a computer is using is stored inside the computer.

WHAT CAN AND CAN'T A COMPUTER DO?

A computer can carry out a sequence of instructions which have been stored inside it. The instructions might include input, processing and output instructions. Processing includes storing and retrieving data, sorting and selecting data, making simple decisions and doing calculations. This is all that a computer can do.

A computer cannot take initiatives, respond to unforeseen circumstances or think for itself.

WHAT EFFECTS ARE COMPUTERS HAVING?

Computers are having both good and bad effects. On the one hand, computers are creating new opportunities. They are extending people's capabilities, taking over monotonous jobs and increasing efficiency. On the other hand, computers are putting some people out of work. They are raising problems about privacy, and making it easier for governments to control people.

To get a better idea of the effects of computers, think of two extreme situations – one where everything is computerised, and the other where there are no computers.

If everything were computerised, unemployment would be very high. The people who control the computers would be very powerful. Everything which we do would be known about, and controlled. It would be an extremely unhealthy situation.

If nothing were computerised, many of the benefits of modern society would disappear. Many banks, factories, businesses and shops would have to close down. Electricity, gas, food and water supplies would be affected. Medical services and the telephone system would be far less efficient. Many people would have to work very long hours doing boring jobs. Life would not be very pleasant.

Obviously, a sensible use of computers is somewhere between these extremes. Deciding just how many computers to use is very difficult.

Only when enough people know about computers can these decisions be made. Perhaps one day you will help to make these decisions.

EXERCISE

1 A person who knows nothing at all about computers asks you 'What is a computer?' How would you answer?

2 Give your own views about how life would be if there were no computers, or if everything were computerised.

3 Discuss, or write about, the question of 'People and Computers'.

4 Some time ago, the following letter appeared in a local newspaper:

> Dear Sir,
> I recently received a telephone bill for £156.72.
> I think it is a disgrace that a few computer operators should be allowed to stop all the telephone bills going out for such a long time. Now I get a huge telephone bill which I can't possibly pay.
>
> The Post Office should go back to having people working out telephone bills. Then it would be done properly.
>
> Yours faithfully,
> P.M. James.

Using your knowledge of computers, write a suitable letter in reply.

5 As you have worked through this book, how has your opinion of the advantages and disadvantages of computers changed?

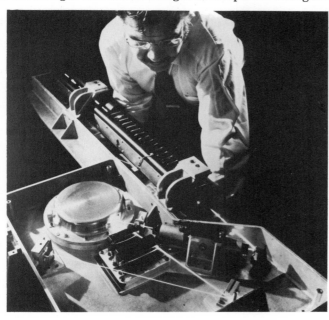

A laser beam printer 151

USEFUL ADDRESSES

The following addresses are useful sources of information about various aspects of computers and computing:

British Computer Society,
13 Mansfield Street,
London, W1M 0BP

National Computer Centre,
Oxford Road,
Manchester, M1 7ED

ICL Computer Education in Schools,
60 Portman Road,
Reading,
Berkshire, RG3 1NR

IBM United Kingdom,
P.O. Box 41,
North Harbour,
Portsmouth,
Hampshire, PO6 3AU

Bank Education Service,
10 Lombard Street,
London, EC3V 9AT

Police National Computer Unit,
Horseferry House,
Dean Ryle Street,
London, SW1

Nascom Minicomputers,
92 Broad Street,
Chesham,
Buckinghamshire, HP5 3ED

Computer Weekly Magazine,
IPC Electrical-Electronic Press Ltd,
Quadrant House, The Quadrant,
Sutton, Surrey, SM2 5AS

Computing Magazine,
53–55 Frith Street,
London W1A 2HG

Computer Education Magazine,
Computer Centre,
North Staffordshire Polytechnic,
Blackheath Lane,
Stafford.

Personal Computer World Magazine,
62a Westbourne Grove,
London, W2

Educational Computing Magazine,
30–31 Islington Green,
London, N1 8BR

Research Machines Limited,
P.O. Box 75,
Oxford,
OX2 0BW

Microcomputer Users in Schools (MUSE),
48 Chadcote Way,
Catshill,
Bromsgrove, Worcestershire, B61 0JT

National Council for Civil Liberties,
186 Kings Cross Road,
London, WC1X 9DE

Amnesty International,
10 Southampton Street,
London, WC2

GLOSSARY

This glossary contains explanations of the technical terms introduced in the text.

abacus	an early calculating device using beads on strings.
accumulator	stores data in the arithmetic and logic unit of a computer.
arithmetic and logic unit (ALU)	part of the central processing unit of a computer, where calculations and logical operations are done.
backing store	storage for large quantities of data outside the central processing unit of a computer.
binary	numbers in base two.
bit	a binary digit, a 0 or a 1.
cell	the storage space in a computer memory for one item of data.
central processing unit (CPU)	the unit of a computer in which processing of data takes place.
chip	see **integrated circuit**.
computer	a machine, controlled by a stored program, which automatically inputs and processes data, and outputs the results of the processing.
computer operator	a person who operates a computer.
control unit	part of the central processing unit of a computer, which controls the step-by-step running of the computer.
counter	a counter controls the number of times a program loop is repeated.
data	information in a form which can be used by a computer.
data bank	a large collection of data.
data processing (DP)	storing, retrieving, sorting or selecting data, changing data from one form into another, doing calculations or making decisions based on data.
dry run	carrying out each step of a program by hand.
ferrite core	a small ring of soft iron which can be magnetised in one direction or the other to store a 0 or a 1.

153

gate	a component which controls the flow of data in a computer.
GIGO	Garbage In, Garbage Out.
hardware	the components and units which make up a computer.
high level language	a programming language designed for a particular use of a computer.
input	to read data or programs into a computer.
input device	a device which reads data or programs into a computer.
integrated circuit	a single circuit which contains a number of transistors and other components.
line printer	an output device which prints one complete line at a time.
loop	a part of a computer program which is repeated a number of times.
low level language	a programming language where each instruction corresponds to one machine language instruction.
machine language	a programming language consisting of instructions in a binary code. The instructions control the hardware of a computer directly.
magnetic tape unit	a device which transfers data to and from magnetic tape.
magnetic disc drive	a device which transfers data to and from a magnetic disc.
main store	see **memory**.
memory	part of the central processing unit of a computer where programs and data are stored.
microcomputer	a computer built up around a microprocessor.
microprocessor	a single integrated circuit containing a complete central processing unit.
operator's console	a device used by a computer operator to send instructions to a computer and the computer to send messages to the operator.
output	to print or display the results of data processing.
output device	a device which prints or displays the results of data processing.
program	a set of instructions to a computer.
programmer	a person who writes and corrects computer programs.
process	an operation, or set of operations, carried out by a computer.
software	another word for **programs**.
system	an assembly of parts functioning as a whole.
terminal	a device providing a direct link between a computer and a person using it.
unit	a piece of equipment which forms part of a computer.
visual display unit (VDU)	a terminal where data is displayed on a screen rather like a television screen.